Babies of the Family

Adebowale Oriku

Pen Press

First published in Great Britain by Pen Press

All paper used in the printing of this book has been made from wood grown in managed, sustainable forests.

ISBN: 978-1-78003-455-3

Printed and bound in the UK
Pen Press is an imprint of
Indepenpress Publishing Limited
25 Eastern Place
Brighton
BN2 1GJ

A catalogue record of this book is available from the British Library

Cover design by Jacqueline Abromeit

We die with the dying:
See, they depart, and we go with them.
We are born with the dead:
See, they return, and bring us with them.

Four Quartets

For the girls: Yejide, Aramide and Simi...

And the boys: Tobi and Tega.

Calvary

I finished writing the essay and went through it a few times before the news came that my sister had cancer and that it may have metastasised. During the weeks before and after the diagnosis, gradually it was borne in on me how in the most desperate moments, fear, superstition, sentimentality and doubt might easily insinuate themselves into the head of someone who prided himself on being deeply imbued with the sensibilities of freethought, ruffle the limpid calm of someone who saw such old 'humane' disciplines as philosophy and literature, and a latter one like psychology, as consolations. With the least pomposity and arrogance I imagined I had risen somewhat above being a blind and shackled captive to at least the first three of the quartet of emotions. As a self-confirmed agnostic, doubt is a given, a necessary quirk, it is my moral business-end. But, after the diagnosis, for six weeks before Adejoke finally succumbed, doubt and a reasonable dollop of fear had pre-empted other emotions.

The essay had nothing to do with cancer. It was one of the occasional secular-minded arguments I set out on a website. It had nothing to do with death either, which might have brought on the unease, the fey underfeeling, that such an article would translate into prescience if my sister's illness ended tragically. The essay, inordinately lengthy and idiosyncratic, was entitled *God Will Not*

Help Nigeria Until… Like most of my articles about religion, God and the eminently godly population of my country of birth, this was written with some degree of petulance – not anger, not condescension. But then any time I decided to write about undue religiosity among Nigerians, some impassioned truth-crunching, a bit of *philosophe*-like preening, helplessness, and even playful irony, always found their way into it. The essay's argument was simple: the title was a quibble. The conclusion was that God – who had momentarily put me in the mind of Samuel Beckett's *Godot* which, or who, probably has nothing to do with God – would certainly not help the country, nor any country for that matter. And why would I stop myself sending out such an article before I even knew my sister was seriously ill?

Now everyone was praying for Adejoke's recovery. The names God and Jesus (and whatever conjurable angels and saints) began to fly like so many arrows trained at the devil and the inevitable 'enemies'. As it dawned on everyone that my sister was not about to turn a corner soon, the intervention of God became imperative. And if I had not become far-gone in agnosticism, I would have been swept into the momentum of votive prayer and the vociferous calling-forth of divine intervention. I was not. I could not. My appetite for the wonderment which religion offers a lot of people had long dulled and I was very much steeped in the ferment of doubt. Besides, I always thought it would be hypocritical and abject to scurry to the corner of my room and offer up prayers in desperation when for more than two decades I had consistently, often openly, questioned the efficacy of prayer and even the existence of the entity to *whom* such prayer was directed.

But such was my love for my sister that I was truly tempted. I wanted to fall on my knees and pray as I had not prayed for decades. It was as if I was being nudged by a kind of force, a galvanising energy, an old shepherd's crook prodding me to appeal to God, to implore Jesus, invoke the intercession of miracle and divine intervention, curry providential favour on behalf of Adejoke. But I stayed true to what I thought was right: to hope as powerfully and as realistically as I could that my sister would get well. And that was even before it was vaguely suggested that what she was suffering from might be cancer. She, of course, was full of prayer herself, in spite of her pain, joining all who had come to visit in fervent praying.

And such was the regard I had for Adejoke's devout and tenacious sense of hope that I could not even bring myself to write and send away new articles, let alone one that questioned the whole of point of religion, prayer and God. For one thing I wasn't being paid for the articles. It was as a displaced, *lumpen* writer in England, with a mind sharp-set for expression and ventilation, that I began to write and send stuff to the website. I began the essay, *God Will Not Help Nigeria Until…*, which I thought would not be more than 1,000 words, a couple of days before Adejoke was admitted to Lagos University Teaching Hospital, after coming in and out of a couple of clinics.

Her admission gave me pause, it unsettled everyone. This might be something serious. A searing pain had invaded her right upper thigh. In the UK, I together with my brother, Dupe, and sister, Folake, were apprehensively following how things were unfolding. Lagos University Teaching Hospital, otherwise called LUTH, was probably the best public service hospital in western Nigeria, if not in the whole country. If a patient was referred to LUTH from some other hospital or clinic, there might indeed be cause for concern. Although the hospital has some of the best medical brains in the world, it is hard to forget or overlook the fact that the Teaching

Hospital might not, comparably speaking, boast gold standard in medicare. If it could, there would not have been any need for the well-off, or those who could afford it, to travel abroad for treatment. Just before Adejoke was admitted to this flagship state hospital in Lagos, the president of the country had just returned to Nigeria to die after months-long sojourn in a Saudi hospital.

My sister's arrival at LUTH was sobering, there was a shadowy half-realisation that we, the siblings, must begin to grapple with unthinkable eventualities. The admission gave a larger ominous dimension to the yet-undiagnosed illness. She was the youngest of already subtracted seven siblings, having lost two before her, a sister and a brother, both older than me. It was unthinkable that any harm – in the shape of a serious illness – should come to Adejoke, so the tempo of prayer reached fever pitch even before the terrible confirmation. The skyline of tangible concrete Yoruba world, as in many African worlds, masses in heavily with the pregnant twilight clouds of the supernatural. When Adejoke's illness was getting into refractory downhill mode, people began to conjure up the invisible hands, claws, fangs and talons of witches, evildoers, wizards and what the ubiquitous evangelicals might call 'principalities'. At this crucial cusp, prayerful friends and well-wishers of Adejoke would come into the hospital ward to conduct prayerthons – gratifying gestures, if they were anything.

I often wonder whether I would have been sucked into the hand-linked circle of hope and faith if I had been there, if I had seen my sister on the hospital bed, suffering. Would I have remained aloof to employing a means whose end a lot of people consider as effective – if not exactly as potent – as medication? After all, even in the balmiest of moments when my mind is not exercised by such mortal perturbations, my 'faith' in science, although huge, is not categorical.

Unquestionably, science is the best that modern man can offer in the way of an understanding of the forces that shape who and what we are, but it is certainly not everything. My transition into an agnostic – or shall we say an irreligious sceptic? – had nothing to do with any triumphalist inebriation with science and its virtues. It had more to do with life and my experiences, as well as a formidable array of self-questionings that no book of philosophy or theology would ever succeed in answering. I do not think anyone comprehends the meaning of the word 'soul' well enough – especially in these days when the 'soul' of the modern man and woman, the computer, the internet technology to be precise, has made utterly bearable the depthless zero-gravity featherlightness of humans – for me to reawaken the dead metaphor of how science might cater for someone's body and religion her soul. Trendier 'Psyche' might be the better word here, particularly in such an inverted backformation as psychology. Besides religion and psychology, other things may be wholesome for the 'soul' or 'psyche.' Literature. Music. Visual Arts. Love. Philosophy. All of these contain trace elements of existential solvent. And that overweening younger sib of psychology: psychoanalysis.

My interest in psychoanalysis and Sigmund Freud dates back to early adolescence – a rather curious and confusing time for Freud to pique anyone's interest. I discovered Freud in a junior encyclopaedia long before I knew what he was getting at. In secondary school we read *Oedipus Rex*, or a Yoruba-world approximation of the Greek tragedy. But Freud was vividly brought home to me by my brother, Akin, who was also my best friend when we were growing up. Akin had shown early promise in fine art. He was so good that my uselessness in art was set in high relief. Of course, I tried to draw, but after a few attempts at some infantile squiggling of simple objects, I gave up completely. And there was a Freudian dimension to the decision. I think what really decided my talentlessness in fine art for me was an unforgettable and rare occasion when Father hunkered down in a corner of wooden floor of our sitting room which the threadbare vinyl floorpiece did not cover and gave us an art lesson of some sort. I was four and Akin was six. In the early 1970s Nigeria, it was rare to see a father giving his children this kind of chummy mini-masterclass. In those days fathers were fathers, patresfamilias, remote, aloof, lordly, undemonstrative and as likely to pillowfight with their children as it would be to find the word 'touchy-feely' in any dictionary at the time. Filial piety was taken with religious gravity. That was probably the only time that Father did anything with Akin and me in a fun way and maybe that is why it remains with me, like a barnacle on a sea-buffeted boulder covering the entrance into the vast cavern of memory. Father, a teacher, passably gifted in line drawing, used a blue-coloured chalk to draw a one-dimensional house with a gabled roof slap on the wood floor and told us to draw what we saw with our own stubs of chalk. Carefully and confidently Akin picked out a façade in a self-assured way, almost as pretty as the one done by Father.

I goofed my way through a bad unpretty copy of the frontispiece, a nonfigurative mare's nest. I messed everything up after that: box, car, tree, face, even the unchallenging stick man. It was easy to blame this on my age, being two years younger than my brother. I was four and Adejoke had not arrived then. I was the last child of the family, technically the 'baby of the family', therefore cosseted enough to be pardoned for being artistically vacuous, with a mind yet unchalked with any promissory markers of talent.

Anyhow, I knew I was never going to be as good as Akin in drawing, which was as far as art went for us then. The beginning of sibling rivalry, *pace* Freud? Well, like many things Freudian, there may be less to it than rivalry. Akin and I became closer throughout primary school years and into secondary school where we were reunited after severally attending different primary schools. There was a Freudian flavour to this too. Both our parents being teachers and often working in separate schools, I, like the boy who tags after his farmer father in Seamus Heaney's poem, *Follower*, had found myself following Father to the schools where he worked and Akin had accompanied Mother. I don't know how our parents came to this arrangement, possibly this was what they had been doing long before it came to our turn and it seemed to be working well – at least for me. There was a kind of pride in being the son of Mr Oriku the Headmaster, far more, I suppose, than being the son of Mrs Oriku, Year Two teacher. It was still years before Mother would become a headmistress, a far less awesome, less grand-sounding title and position than headmaster – and of course 'headmistress' was considerably defanged by its femininity. In my last term in primary school, Father was 'transferred' to another school.

The thing about Freud is that any relationship children have with their parents could be mined for overt attachments, invidious preferences or hidden conflicts and every sort of dusty hole-and-corner impurity – he would root for all this too in the relationship with siblings. Now wasn't it Freudian that my interest in literature and the ambition to be a writer, a fine artist of words, a painter of verbal images, compensation for my inability to be a visual artist? And there was an argument

I once had with a friend, even before I put a word down in a literary way, when I was about 16. I contended that between the triarchy of the arts, writing was the most supreme, the most regal, first among equals. Fela Kuti's music might be superb; a painting by Rembrandt sublime; but Shakespeare or Soyinka (I had just read Soyinka's *The Man Died* then, a book legendary among impressionable Nigerian youths for being a marvel of grammar and vocabulary) were greater artists. This could only have come from the unconscious, a Freudian analyst might say, that with an inner eye set to becoming a writer, I tried to presume some sort of superiority over my brother and his talents. And a tapestry of unresolved complexes could be woven out thus, even down to the fact that Akin had won first prize during a 'baby show' before I was born, that this was a profound internecine sibling rivalry.

It is not difficult to see why Freud is loathed by some; or if not exactly loathed, why he is seen as loathsomely hyperbolic (with words like hysterical and hypothetical also coming to mind interchangeably) in the pitching of his ideas or even in his methodology. Freud is seen as essentially wide of the mark in many of his postulations, as too speculative and monomaniacal in tying everything up, or rather unravelling everything, with sex. When he was about 15 and I 13, Akin explicitly introduced the sexual Freud into our lives. One day he brought home a black-and-white print of a picture in which the spectacled profile of a man's head was frontally silhouetted with the image of a limberly reclining woman, an upthrust leg tracing the nose, the pubic hair picking out the eyebrow, the bosom describing the forehead. The picture's caption was *What's on a Man's Mind – Sigmund Freud.* I wasn't a man yet and what *is* on a man's mind should not be any business of mine, but I think I saw what the person called Freud was getting at, having assumed that Freud himself drew the picture. Akin put up the risqué poster on the wall of the room we shared, in the middle of the back wall somewhere between our separate beds, it was the first thing that anyone entering the room would see, arrestingly so. For some two years or thereabouts he pencilled several dozen copies of the print, giving many to friends and, still very much taken with the picture, he just sketched and resketched for the fun of it, and at last we added two pencil-drawn ones of the pop-arty duplications with the original print on the wall.

And perhaps it was no less a Freudian matter that just about that time I began to doodle words on paper, in corners of newspapers, in spaces and gaps between book pages and even, occasionally, on walls, the beginnings of what I would later self-define with the medievalese, *furor scribendi*: writing fury or mania. The picture Akin brought home and propagated exemplifies what people think is wrong with Freud, his seeming fixation with sex, his sprinkling of the unconscious with a million moral pathogens and his belief that psychoanalysis was science. Psychoanalysis might just as well be pseudoscience or anything Freud's critics wish to call it and a work like *Interpretation of Dreams* might truly be a screed written by a fantasist, weighted with every sort of fancy, but his short essay called *Mourning and Melancholia* is perhaps the most insightful contribution to the subject of loss, grief, the trauma of mourning and bereavement. Some time before Ȧdejoke fell ill I had bought and read *The New Black* by Darian Leader – the slim book a sensible elaboration on Freud's paper.

However, most of the psychoanalytical books that I had been reading before my sister's illness were by authors of Jungian persuasion, having found my way to them through Jung himself (in other words what I had been reading was analytic psychology). My discovery of

Jung was early too, actually coincident with knowing Freud. One cannot read a thumbnail vignette of Sigmund Freud's life without being introduced to Carl Gustav Jung, a younger man, a fellow psychoanalyst who fell out with the older man to establish his own school whose name was inverted as Analytic Psychology. Freud's overemphasis on the role of sexuality – particularly its repression – was at the heart of the parting of the two men.

My interest in the works of these two men has always been more than cursory, I have found myself returning to them and to works by authors who belong in either – or both – camps. And while Freudian sexual subsets like 'Castration Complex' have only provided me with comic raw material when writing a sceptical – and inevitably scabrous – skit on Jesus' advice to cut off any part of one's body that is making one sin, I think there is more to the bulk of the Freud's work than he is being given credit for today.

In the last days of Adejoke's illness, naturally she had turned more inwards. She dreamt a lot: deep, meaningful, meaningless, symbolic and sometimes frightening dreams. I could not help but recall Jung, whose own interpretation and appreciation of dreams I found more relevant to the situation than Freud's, to my own almost devotional reflection on the past and the wistful memories of sibling relationship with my sister. Even so, when I decided not to publish my opinion on whether or not God can help any country to develop when my sister was ill, it had nothing to do with the gnostic ideas of C G Jung, his dead-set equation of the divine with the unconscious, his description of atheism as a 'stupid error' and an 'urban neurosis'. Nor did his *Answer to Job* – which exquisitely treats the complex nature of an amoral God who is selfish, mad, bad, dangerous, unreliable but ultimately redemptive – help me understand why my younger sister should languish and suffer for no reason other than being biologically 'selected' to be a martyr to an illness. Of course, Jung provides insights, brilliant philosophical syntheses about the 'dual' nature of God, but this does not detract from his inveterate godmindedness, even godliness, in his belief in the ineffable transcendence. This should be commended in someone who dreamt, when he was a boy of 11, of seeing the image or apparition of God defecating on the Basel Cathedral. But then it is one thing to dream of God defecating on a cathedral and another to imagine God not caring a damn about shitting on humanity in varied doses – which is pretty much the agnostic angle. Atheists will not shift ground from the position that the whole idea of God is bullshit, the atheist comedian, George Carlin, says as much in his 'Religion is Bullshit' routine.

But even as I mothballed the article, wishing that Adejoke would get well as soon as possible, without too much suffering, I could not help wondering whether this was a veiled prayer. Of course, I stopped writing altogether when I saw she had not improved. Hope and bemusement concentrated my mind, and there was this flickering of anger. Wasn't that *the* fear of God of sorts? Would I have published the article if I had thought about other things besides belief, religion and the ruinous effect of the overdoing of both? Even if I did not fear the wrath of God, wasn't I supposing that an article, written by the brother of a victim of God's fickle ways, would be counterintuitive? Counterintuitive in whose eyes?

After all it was not likely that any of those who would read the article would know that my sister was ill, nor would it have meant much to them if they knew. Being a writer of some kind, introspection has always been close to the surface, egoless self-assessment is something I know I am capable of, the ability to ask myself, for instance, how genuinely irreligious I am, how authentically sceptical I have become. I know I am not beyond letting out 'Jesus!' or 'Oh my God!' every now and then. During conversations with family and friends, references to God, God's infinite power, mercy, justice and a fatalistic resignation which hinges on God's whim are so common as to be natural, but for me the word God now signifies nothing. I think the sort of atavistic need which made early man and woman stumble unto religion has also ensured that God as an ideal, an idea, is now almost synonymous with the 'collective unconscious', even in those who say they do not believe. For more than two decades, the necessity to say the word God, and what 'He' can do when someone is ill, or even as a metaphor for an elixir, or as the symbol of the ultimate corrective, has been completely removed from me. It just does not come naturally to me again, and even when I let slip, I do it self-consciously, no more than a lip-deep expletive.

My writing is another matter. Since I started to write, I have never found any need to bring up God's name as *the* solver of problems, nor as the creator of them in the first place. I've always kept my feet on the ground, more so with my latter conviction that things are so arbitrary in the way they happen that even if there were a being overseeing it all, he must be arbitrary too. Avoiding appeals to God in what I write has shown me how natural and necessary it is for some to declaim how God may be the only thing that can help Nigeria solve its multitudinous problems. I noticed this (pathetic) fallacy a long time ago, even before the country became church-ridden, a veritable God-yard, before the repetition of the word God reached the morbid stage reminiscent of a sufferer from *echolalia*, that disorder in which one repeats everything someone else says.

My essays about the practice of religion on the website were never popular, although the click-count might show that several hundred people had read or glanced over them. It was often clear that some who read the articles would love to string me up, or maybe burn me at the stake, or throw me into the pit straight away – at the very least it kindled flame wars of sorts. I may even have lost an old university friend, a long-lost schoolmate that I re-found through the Internet, when he read my 'irreligious' articles. He was an assistant pastor of an evangelical church and he seemed to have woken up slowly to the fact that the easygoing, open-minded classmate of his had become passionately anticlerical and unashamedly antitheist (both of which I am not, in a definitive sense). Such a reaction to my articles meant pretty much nothing to me. Without any scruple, I was prepared to sacrifice an Internet-revived friendship, or even the friend himself, on the altar of common sense. So I continued to write the occasional essay or article that made counterleaps from religious faith and showed how faith, when it is unmediated with thought and a dash of doubt, turns the existential human blindness that led to it in the first place into utter purblindness.

I could write several essays in a month about what our faddish and breathless infatuation with religion – a rather earthbound species of religion – was doing to the country and how religion was being over-celebrated in Nigeria, but I always, unconsciously, checked myself from doing this. And I do not think this had anything to do with what some might easily impute as vestigial embers of religious belief in me, that at the core of my being, I might as well be a closet Christian, a bewildered believer, still seduced by the blandishments of religion, and that I was only trying to find my way back to the flock. I got into a costive mode and hesitated at sending articles that questioned what most of those who would read them believed in because of the likelihood of becoming a yowling yawn, something far worse than a crashing bore. For one thing, I was conscious that the essays would have little or no impact – or they might only impact in the way of several wishful and fevered imaginings of me being flung into hell!

Just before it was tentatively confirmed that Adejoke had cancer, I mustered the will to return to *God Will Not Help Nigeria Until…*, reread it again and again, to detect anything that might constitute a mockery of the chorus of prayer at my sister's bedside in faraway Lagos. The article was overlong, a few hundred chastening words had exploded into an essay of several thousand. Then I realised how my feelings about religion and its facile practice among Nigerians had caused me to run away with words, almost 4,000 words of mock-apostolic confutation of the role religion and God in the life of a country, or even a person, and this was when I ran into the passage that pitched me into a headspin: *As it is, 'personal relationships' between God and his creatures have always been so fraught that someone who is patently 'sinless', or rather 'righteous' with bits of venial sins (whatever that means), might find himself in the grip of a cancerous calvary which no medicine or prayer would be able to assuage, which may have called forth the convoluted obfuscation, or consolation, of God's ways being mysterious.*

I wrote the above maybe two weeks before my sister went into LUTH. When people talk about hindsight and retrospection, the words are rarely allied with foresight and prognostication, they usually come with regrets, irreversible errors, missteps and nostalgia. But when I was writing these words, the farthest thing from my mind was that a week later Adejoke would enter that horrific state of 'calvary' – or less figuratively, the state of pain and suffering. I winced and felt slightly dizzy when I read the passage again, the oracular weight of it. Where did these thoughts come from? Of course it was a flat, even unoriginal, statement whose truthfulness was as self-evident as 'Every human must die'. Human beings suffer needlessly – unless there is any good reason unknown to us that an innocent tot should perish with her young family in a road accident. But why and whence did I conjure up cancer and its relentless, prayer-defying depredations? Mere reasoning? Serendipity? Jungian 'synchronicity' (an idiosyncratic rarefied name for coincidence)? Or was it what physicists might call 'quantum entanglement' slightly disentangled from its technical sense? Any one of these might be as true as the other. But, sincerely, those words in the essay were not strictly written off-the-cuff, some reflection went into bringing them out, some thought; although it could easily have been straightforward agnostic adlibbing. Millions of people are laid low, cut down, by cancer every year – so it might as well be a piece of impersonal reasoning. However, there was someone in the corner of my mind, crouched in the twilit backdrop of the memory, when I wrote the words, someone as dear and close to me as Adejoke. In 2001, my brother, Femi, the one who came before Akin, had died of cancer.

And when, a decade later, it was confirmed that Adejoke also had cancer, I 'prayed' in the best way someone like me could – tersely, poetically, introspectively:

Do not go at all dear sister,
but if you must do not go before me.
Do not take leave. Let's plead with time.

Do not take wing so early – or aren't you
still nature's fledgling, a sapling in bloom?
Sister, sister-german... Stay!

Battles and Wars

It is curious how things turn out, even things one might believe are trivial and not worthy of a moment's consideration. Femi came into the world two years after a girl, Folake, the Independence Baby, because she was born during the year of Nigeria's independence. Maybe being of different genders, Folake and Femi never became playmates in the way Akin and I did – loving siblings like us all, but not playmates. And why not Femi and Akin, who were only separated by as many years (a couple) as me and Akin? Even now I can't easily explain this. It was not as if Femi had become lonely as a result of this, he was perhaps the most gregarious of us brothers, from the early days he had no problem cultivating and keeping friends. In a cool noiseless sort of way, he was a guy about town. Somehow Akin and I had come to see him as a caring 'big brother', and he had the temperament and protective good nature to sustain this.

Just as I think that Adejoke, even if she were a boy, would not have become as close a playmate as Akin to me. She was born almost five years after I was born, a year after the Nigerian Civil War. I, for my part, came right at the start of the war. I was the War Child. I was born a few days into the Nigerian Civil War. The war broke out on 6th July and I arrived four days later. In the parturitional calendar I could have been born any time within a week of the start of the war. Mother had even told me later that she began to feel the oncoming a few days before the war and that the night before the declaration, I seemed set to come out but that the next morning, before and after the war was declared, I had become unusually calm, motionless, and had remained so for a couple of days. Mother was worried. What is going on? Why is it not kicking, turning and hiccupping – something she said I did a lot inside – overgulping the fluid maybe? But then again I had kicked, turned and hiccupped, and possibly burped, and some hours later I came out.

Naturally the 'happy event' was muted. The country was at war, and there was no song and dance. Mother told me that a few days after I was born, she woke up one night and put on the bedside light in the room to quieten my colicky cries with bottled milk because somehow I seemed to be unsatisfied with suckling. A staccato burst of martial voices wafted up to her in the upstairs room and the disembodied barks of soldiers commanded whoever put on the light to put it off. As had been enjoined a few days before, every glazed window in every house should be sealed with cardboard or carton or kraft paper, no lights must be seen from the street, every light must be baffled, or even snuffed, every sound killed, even baby cries must be muffled, or the baby muzzled if that would keep it quiet.

It was in this bated atmosphere that I was born. When I was growing up, some relatives called me Bogunde – *He who comes with war*. Although she did not always object, it was apparent that Mother did not like the epithet. If I had turned out as a tiny terror, a toddling incarnation of a poltergeist, screeching, breaking and smashing everything up in the house, perhaps Mother would have told people outright to stop calling me *He who comes with war*, she would not have forgotten the

Yoruba saying that a name inevitably becomes its bearer. It was one thing to be born in the time of a grave crisis – a lot of children must even have been born on the day of the declaration of war – it was another to become homonymous with war. And even with an eye to the future, Mother would not have wanted the name to stick. On the physical level, it wouldn't be funny for someone to tell their daughter, for instance, that her boyfriend whose name was *He who comes with war* was at the door. And the name would have become me if I grew up to be fractious or grumpy or even bellicose, then *He who comes with war* had truly come with war.

Anyway, the name did not stick. Before I reached adolescence no one called me Bogunde again. It slipped away with the receding memory of the Civil War. In 2000, when I was working as a journalist in the Gambia, I recalled the name Bogunde in an elegiac essay I wrote about the 40th year of Nigeria's independence, and how being born at the start of the Nigerian Civil War made me an 11th-hour child of sorts, an arrival preludial to a very long and dark night. Years before, when I was penning away at just about anything that took my fancy, a time when the scribbling fury that I mentioned in the first chapter had thrown up a mania for poem-making, I scribbled dozens of poems, ditties, haikus, orikus and a number of amphigouris. I will repeat *Bellum Baby* here.

Mother, the first quickening is a warning,
the tiny twitch that begins it all? The tic
in your tummy – a warning, forewarning.
I can see the war as clear as amnio-fluid,
clear as crystal, I know it is coming,
I see it all thru the guts, mine and yours, thru
the tortuous umbilicus, I see the bearded colonel
from the east belching fury, bent on battle,
having a while made Sun Tzu's Art of War his bible.

I see the beardless baby-faced colonel straddling
the north and west, bent
on returning fire, primed by a mantra
of keeping everything, everyone, together
at any cost, at all costs.
The war will be big and bad, Mother,
long-drawn-out and sad, a mad mad war,
and when I cease to 'kick' it's truly calm
before a storm, stock-taking silence, unabated
stillness, but unlike me, Biafra will be deadborn
and aborted and Lugardland will remain as it is.
As you know, Mother, there are other wars
to fight, other battles to battle out.
Okay, the crag-faced Irish sage may have
overblown it: you are not going to birth
me over a grave, but the truism
is yet true – I will retrace my steps, or
shamble my way, to the grave anyway.
Meanwhile the wars, the battles!
And let's be honest I don't see
any point in waxing poetic about this now.
I am bored already, weary, world-weary...

I remember imagining what Freud, or his followers, would make of the poem, its Oedipal longings, regression even beyond childhood to foetus, the escapism, an id-born poem that struggles to calibrate itself into normalcy with the ministrations of the ego – and how the super-ego had succeeded in teasing humour out of the supposedly dark subject. Or wasn't I grieving at the time I wrote it? Was I? And there is my first experience of war, one in the string of figurative wars that life is saddled with: the tiffs, the troubles, problems, life's many wars, small and big, physical and spiritual. The wars we wage against one another, which are pretty minor more often than not. The behemoth wars nature wages against us, blindfold cosmic wars, as forbidding and as potentially damaging and destructive as the vast whirling blades of a thousand windmills inhabited by a deathless monstrous ogre and its clones who were all variously cranking them up, to disorientate and derange us, and our pitiably Quixote-like efforts to lash back. And if life is an endless chain of wars then we must all be warriors of sorts. I do not know how the word battleaxe came to be a metaphor for a belligerent, formidable, everlastingly cross woman, but it so happened that the first real battle that I had in life seemed to have been with a young version of what a male chauvinist comic might call a 1960s feminist: a battleaxe. But before the battle there was a skirmish with what, for want of a more apt term, I shall call fate, or maybe vicarious hubris.

All through my primary school years I enjoyed a kind of sheltered, semiprivileged life. As I followed Father from one primary to another, I did not fully grasp the substance this had given me, the stamp of separateness and exclusivity which other pupils may have envied. The tag of the 'Son of the Headmaster' had followed me from school to school. Things like journeying to school and back in my father's Morris or Opel counted for much, not trudging on dirt and asphalt unsandalled like other pupils. More significantly, during lunchtime break I always sauntered into Headmaster's Office to polish off my meal while other pupils went to two middle-aged women selling food in the shade of a tree in a corner of the school playground. Usually the school's Senior Girl would go round to the food sellers to pick up a prepaid, modestly-portioned plate of food – usually rice and broth-thin fish stew – and bring it to the office for me where I waited like a kind of slightly paupered princeling.

Although Father always told me to go out immediately after finishing my meals to play with friends, I often preferred to stay in the office flipping through books on the table, browsing atlases and sundry charts and teacherly posters on the wall. I would pick a stray newspaper, skim through the stories, or read a storybook I had brought along, sometimes uninterestedly overhearing what Father and the deputy headmaster were saying, usually stuff about 'school's board', Teachers' Union, a trying teacher and so forth. I was a rather introspective child, rather studious, calmly curious about things, and somehow I found myself coming top of my class. I always won prizes for taking the 'first' position in end-of-term examinations. During the end-of-year last day's assemblies I was always called to the podium to accept the prizes, and this had further given my stature as Headmaster's Son greater robustness. In my fifth and penultimate year in primary school, Mother briefly acted as deputy to Father before she went away to head another school, and during this brief period in which my mother and father were running the school together, Akin was there too, in final year. He went into secondary school just as Mother went to head another school and Adejoke had replaced Akin as Mother's follower.

In my final year in primary school, I was again left with Father, still demurely basking in my status as Headmaster's Son. I was in Class Six A, the stream occupied by brainier pupils, actually by a rainbow of bright to merely adequate pupils, pupils of both poster and pastel academic shades. Mr Adekunle was the class teacher, styled as Mr A, and no one could say whether the A stood for the initial of Adekunle or Class Six A because Mr Adekunle had been teaching Class A for some 12 years before I arrived there. He considered the class a special one, the *sanctum sanctorum* to every classroom in the school, the hub; he'd farced up the class's gravitas since he started to teach it. He considered the class an island of excellence within a sea of educational common-or-garden, or maybe the other way round, a dune-shaded oasis in a desert of perfunctory sameness. He called Class Six A 'the Lyceum' – in the Aristotelian sense, that is – because Mr A was partial to throwing Greek and Latin words and terms into his sentences, often English sentences composed of Latinate-sounding words. Since the cream of the cream of pupils in the three arms of Year Five always ended up in Six A, Mr A often had a reasonable number of fairly clued-up pupils he could rely upon to achieve his pedagogical end. In the class of about 30, only ten pupils often mattered to Mr A, the best, the smartest, the cerebral, the bright sparks, he treated them specially. Then there are the ten in the middle, often treated in a lukewarm way, with a kind of vaguely hopeless disinterest. I believe Mr A was not under any impression that the middle ten would cross the line to the best ten, although he could not care less whether they stayed in the halfway limbo or crossed the line into bottom ten. These last ten were the dregs of the class, frass, dross, these were the lowbrow pupils, over against the middlebrow and the favoured highbrow. Mr A did not hide the disregard in which he held this bottom ten pupils, he treated them with rank uninterest.

Now to be fair to Mr A, he did not divide the class overtly, not with any Euclidean simplicity, nor had he made up any crudely pseudo-Darwinian pigeonholing of the children's abilities. It was only that if the law of averages was applied, what one would arrive at was such a fractional maths. Clearly, Mr A had his favourites, the *Alpha* pupils. And there were those in the middle who may have been caught between *Mu* and *Nu*. Then there was a great leap to the *Omega* pupils, because Mr A wasted no time in throwing such words as Dunderhead and Tomfool at about eight of the pupils in the class, pupils who were not quick to answer questions or who would think twice before putting up their hands. Although it was likely that even the least competent of Mr A's tomfools would be better than any pupil in Class Six B, he just could not be bothered, he could not suffer slowness in his pupils. Normally he taught the whole class together and he would have honestly wished that everyone was getting it, but I think he had decided that there were some who would not get it, no matter what effort he made. Then there were those who would get it even before he said anything, and among the good ones he had his star pupil, the genius among the brainies, the polymath pupil who knew everything even beyond what he was taught, the *dux* before whom the dunces must kowtow.

Mr A was a charismatic young man of about 35, neither short nor tall, neither big nor small. He always appeared neatly nifty and it was likely that outside of school he would make freer with sartorial indulgence than the somewhat regulation garb he wore to school. Even then he was the most refreshingly dressed among the male teachers: well-ironed drainpipe trousers that recalled the 1950s, cuff-linked shirts of loose primary colours, often offset with mute-toned cravats. The black shoes, always laced, glancingly polished. The carefully barbered hair, cropped low at the sides and back of the head and bevelled into a low-slung puff towards the front, a tasteful, if quaint, alternative to the Afro which was the rage then. The very dark sunglasses which Mr A never forgot to wear, a fixture on his face. And a tuft of well-trimmed minion beard. To call attention to himself Mr A often hawked in a curtly deliberate way, and it might signify anything from mild indignation to simmering irritation with a dunderhead which might lead to a whispery 'Bring me my cudgel'. I still do not know why Mr A preferred the word cudgel to 'cane' or even to 'whip', except for his proclivity towards archaism. Cudgel was verbal overkill for the wand-sized cane which the teacher used to strike the open palm of those he needed to chide with anything more than words, but often words were enough, cutting comments on a pupil's inability to learn. And it might just be for the sound of the word cudgel or how Mr A had chosen to enunciate it: cuud-giil. Even decades later, the euphonious, schoolmasterish flair and drama with which the word escaped Mr A's mouth still amuses, it recalls to me the word 'strigil', the sickled blade used in ancient Rome to scrape dirt and sweat from the skin after bathing or exercise.

I was one of those who were spared Mr A's cudgel. I was, of course, one of the academically 'elect', for this was a classroom in which Jesus' ironising of the last turning out to be the first – or the other way round – did not apply. Although not quite Gradgrindian in temperament, Mr A would mentally pat the head of a pupil who was able to define a horse as precisely and as eloquently as possible. I was one of those who would get the definition down to a tee. Mr A had been following my scholastic career for several terms, for the two years my father had been headmaster of the school. He would have noticed that I was invariably winning first-place prizes during end-of-term examinations, and this must have wowed him. It was a matter of course that I would be placed in his Class 6 A, but even if by some reason there was to be a random placement in the two classes of year six, Mr A would have fought fiercely to see me in his class. He would have done anything: begged, cajoled, bribed and headhunted with all the will he had. I knew all this because he had made glowing remarks about my performance to my father.

I could see the glint in Mr A's eyes, I felt his exhilaration for having me in his class, he could not hide his self-satisfaction, even from me. I was his prize pupil, the super-catch in his ozonic catchment. Just as Mr A had what he called a 'scapegrace' among his perceived underachievers, he also had the 'star' pupil among the achievers – the sole overachiever, beyond reproach, beyond disgrace. It was clear from the first who he wanted to make his star pupil. The teacher had this vintage manner of calling everyone by their surname, and the first time he called out my name in the class he couched it in a kind of classical cognominal portentousness that seemed to warn the class of the intellectual force of nature in their midst: ORIKU.

Mr A had a mock-Montessori way of testing his pupils. He'd write out a problem on the blackboard and would begin to call out pupils to come to the front of the class to solve it, and for reasons easily understandable, he liked to set cloze tests in almost every subject he taught. For instance, in an English language class he might write out a sentence far more complex and elided than this example, *He likes ... cat*, and he would then offer the options of *his* or *her* as a filler, or in geography class he would write, *The capital of Ghana is ...*, giving the option of *Lagos* and *Accra*. Mr A would then start by calling out a pupil he called a dunderhead or tomfool every now or then and would tell him (often a boy) to take a piece of chalk and fill in the answers, knowing full well that the tomfool was likely to fluff it. Or if, by any chance, the tomfool got it right or any of the two or three pupils he called after the tomfool, he would crank up the odds and write out a more complex sentence. In a geography class, he might ask what the capital of Nepal was or the largest city and capital city of Brazil, respectively. He knew he was asking difficult questions because he had not even taught the class some of the things. Mr A's intention was to handpick five or six pupils from the groups he considered as average and less than average and when they had all got the question wrong, he would then call out one of his top boys and girls to solve the problem. More than half of the time his star pupil was the last child he would call, the *deus ex machina* in this lopsided assessment. Mr A would sit back, relaxed in goggled sphinxhood, indulging himself in a kind of understated kibitzing. In the first week, I played my role swimmingly. Mr A had successful used me to show up some of my classmates, and for a ten-year-old this was either something to be proud of or something that was not worthy of consideration. I really did not know what it meant to spare someone's feelings, and I thought it could not be wrong or bad if I was used as a foil for dunderheads.

At the start of the second week Mr A wrote a mathematical problem on the blackboard. He was particularly impatient with dunderheads that morning and had called out two pupils who might at last succeed in solving the problem, but had given them short shrift. With a kind of self-assurance he had not displayed before, he called me out: 'Oriku, come and show these tomfools how to do it.' Unknown to Mr A, even before he called me my heart had sunk right into one of my feet, so much that the extremity might as well have become leaden with elephantiasis, or weighted with clay. But I mustered some strength and sidled towards the blackboard, my heart leaping back to its cage to beat and throb like many hammers of a glockenspiel. I arrived before the blackboard, picked up a piece of chalk limply, and then I just froze. No, I hadn't suddenly been stricken with catatonia or any other condition that might induce inertia and speechlessness. I had, since I was in year five or so, begun to recognise that I was turning out as pretty shit in mathematics, a realisation which became starker that year when the simple arithmetic of early primary school morphed into mathematics. Up to year five I could still manage to score 70 or even 80 percent in arithmetic, but the groundwork of my apathy towards maths had been laid even as I got to that school. And what has been described as the 'Pygmalion Effect' also failed the teacher that morning: his altitudinous expectation and the projection of airtight omniscience on me did not make me even start to chalk anything up. Whenever I remember this debacle, the pun 'Polymathy sans maths' never fails to rear its frightful, sardonic head. But Mr A had missed this chink in what he thought was the ironclad repleteness of my academic wizardry. We were both caught up in coils of fortune like Robert Burns' 'mouse' and 'man', but even now I wonder which was man and which was mouse between Mr A and me. Didn't I need to offer an apology to the trusting teacher for upsetting his tidy, well-laid-out assumption about me? I shuffled back to my seat, confused and cobweb-headed. It was as if I had been coshed hard on the head, the grey stuffing knocked out of me, replaced with loops of cobweb, gossamer – or with clay, I had become clod-pated. Mr A was crestfallen. He harrumphed darkly and lengthily, his star pupil had failed to shine on that Monday morning, had indeed fallen from on high. In the firmament of the teacher's imagination I had exploded like a meteoroid. Or was it a temporary lapse? Monday malaise?

The reason I was able to sustain a prime position until I got to his class was something that simple arithmetic could solve in mere number value, or addition, or what in mathematics itself might come under number theory in integers (and what's the difference between 'number value' and 'number theory,' or arithmetic and mathematics, or even six and half-a-dozen?). Even if I scored as low as 50 in mathematics, the full percentages that I always got in seven or eight other subjects would more than compensate for this middling mark. Sometimes I still wonder how Mr A felt that morning, how disappointed and embarrassed, even perplexed, he would have been, and whether, proud man that he was, he would have taken anything from the experience. He never called me out again to solve any mathematical problem, even he became circumspect about calling me to solve other problems in other subjects, and within a few weeks he stopped calling pupils out. Again I wondered whether the teacher had completely squelched or merely scotched the belief he had in me, whether he'd turned off or merely toned down the candlepower of the halo he'd lit around me. And I was happy that my father soon left the school. In the last two terms that I spent in primary school, my father was not the school's headmaster. For some reason he was 'transferred' to another school, and now he thought it would not be necessary for me to follow him. He'd told Mr A to keep an eye on me, act in *loco parentis*, give tutelage beyond mere teaching.

But even Mr A couldn't have saved me from the girl who might as well be a budding battleaxe. The biggest and the last battle I had in primary school happened on the last day of my final year. In the evening of the last day of every school year, there was always a kind of vaudeville show, otherwise dubbed a 'concert'. On the evening of a concert, playlets would be staged, often cautionary and morality sketches, there were also madrigalesque renditions and choreographed choral music. Every pupil looked forward to the concert, I did too. For the year six pupils it was also a valedictory event, a kind of rite-of-passage ceremony, preliminary to secondary school world and adolescence.

After Father left the school, a group of boys, some of them bullies, took it upon themselves to form a sturdy wall of protection around me. I was a weedy-looking, vulnerable-seeming slip of a boy. But perhaps more for being a book-reading lone wolf from as early as I can remember than my stature, I was never into any schoolground roughhousing nor would I deign to pick a fight with any pupil. Somehow the fact that my father was headmaster and that I had not let that get into my head – possibly combined with my somewhat bookish gifts – had endeared me to most of the boys in my class. Although no one would describe me as a chatterbox, my chats with the boys were often characterised with imagination and elfish effervescence. Whenever I sat with the boys, story after story would spill from my mouth. I often found myself regaling them with the more heady overwrought tales and snippets from the books and encyclopaedias that I had read, usually overembroidered and vivified with colour. Two of the boys I got close to were Mr A's dunderheads, and though dunderhead they might be, they had the clout and presence to take over the running of the class whenever Mr A was not around, muscling aside the class captain, whom they considered the teacher's toady, an all-round brilliant boy and an embryonic mathematical genius, doggedly methodical and seriously unplayful. In the second and last term of the final year, he beat me to the first position in the examinations, scoring as high in mathematics as in other subjects. Although I still went up the podium to collect prizes, they were given for being second best, silver prizes. I had slipped from being *numero uno* to being *proxime accessit* (which was how Mr A would put it). I never begrudged the boy his accomplishments. In those early childhood days, the father of the liberal-minded man in me had been born, it didn't bother me being second, although I don't know how I would feel if I suddenly became one of Mr A's slackers. And even though I never had anything against Mr A for putting so much trust in me, after the anticlimax of the proscenium display of my mathematical fecklessness, I understood a bit of what those at the receiving end of Mr A's behaviour were going through. Somehow I found myself gravitating towards this sort of boys, the potentially streetwise rather than schoolwise, the more devil-may-care among them.

Everyone would get their report cards after the noon-time school assembly. Then all pupils would leave for home to prepare for the late-afternoon concert, take off their school uniforms and wear their Sunday best if they had any. Before, I would not have needed to walk home, I would have waited for Father to finish whatever he was doing, ride home in his car and then return with him later for the concert. But now I had to walk like other pupils – and I liked it that way, especially for the banter. On the last day, as usual I joined a ragtag group of bad boys and the class's run-of-the-mill. We got to the school's sizable and alopecian football pitch. A path ran through the side of the pitch straight to the school's gateless entrance. After-school fights were common, this was the time a bad boy might have to confront another bad boy from another class, or just someone from a rival group. And there were the plain bullies looking for butts to rattle and sometimes beat up. So the butts, who often forgot that bullies might find one reason or the other to pick a fight with them, were ambushed on the way, given a raw deal, especially on such a mildly anarchic day as the last day of the term when everything would have been forgotten before the school resumed. There was a group of bad girls and one or two she-bullies; they did pretty well the same thing as the boys. Whenever a group of bad girls and bad boys crossed each other's path there was often a sparring exchange of taunts, catcalls, hissing, hackle-raising, bristling and bridling. There was never really any physical clash between the boys and the girls.

As I walked with the swaggering bad boys, we suddenly discovered that a group of girls were some distance ahead of us, their piping prepubescent voices raised to a kind of jarring sopranette pitch. The boy who was considered the leader of our group, stockier but no taller than any of us, had yelled in a voice he would have loved to register and impinge like a thug's cultivated gutturalism, but which had come out shrilly, castrato-like: 'Fatso!' He repeated the scream: 'Fatso!' Fatso was the tallest and biggest girl among the girl-group. 'Fatso Number One', the boy yelled again, making it more pointed, more acute, because a couple of the girls were indeed fat. The girls stopped, turned around. We stepped nearer and stopped too. There began an exchange of abuses. I stepped well back, though, I wasn't used to this sort of thing. But when a whelp-like boy shouted, 'Bloated Wet Bread' to the leader of the group of cattish girls, I allowed a giggle to escape my mouth and the big bad girl turned on me, picking me out from where I stood in the background.

'Oh, you've become one of these fools. You skinny nitwit. Your father is no more the headmaster now, so I can say what I like to you.'

The big girl could answer back to the other boys, but it seemed she had had it in for me for some time, and truly at the time Father was headmaster, no pupil would try what the girl had done. But I did not say a word, I didn't know anything about schoolground cut-and-thrust.

The fat girl continued nevertheless: 'You have become the puppy of the big dog here.' The big dog was the leader of the pack of us boys. 'And you have the guts to yip when the dog yapped,' or something to that effect.

Now the boys had made way for me and one of them had nudged me to step towards the girl. As I walked charily and hesitantly towards the girl, in a rather belated, forced, thinly alliterative appeasement of Momus, I breathed: 'Fat fool.'

With a quick movement of her chunky limb, the little Amazon made a long arm for me, intending to box my head. But I deflected the assailment of the soft-boned flesh in a self-surprising dance of reflex. My friends, the boys, cried, beginning with an innocent double-entendre: 'Give it to her, Ade. Teach her a lesson she will take to secondary school.' A circle had now been formed around me and the girl. The gymslipped girls were also urging their friend to go for it. She closed with me, lashing out with her meaty fists. But with a presence of mind that could only have sprung from desperation, from a momentary desire not to be crushed by the seemingly boneless fists of the girl, I crouched reflexively, reached out my arms and arced them round her legs, pretty much grazing the calves. Her fall was easy, ludicrous, almost gravity-defying. I looked down at the girl as she lay spread-eagled, face-up, puffing in a corner of the turf. And then I had done something that I would immediately regret. The girl was struggling to pick herself up, but urged by my friends' hoots and baying, which had dwarfed the damped whining of the girls, I suddenly found myself sitting on her, pummelling her face with my slinky fists. After half a dozen hits, my friends pulled me up and tossed me on their shoulders, chanting: 'Hail Ade. Hail Ade. You've given her a good send-off.'

Somehow the girls still managed to reply, settling for the last word: 'You should all be ashamed of your coward friend. He has only defeated a girl in a fight and you carry him on your shoulders. Wimps.'

My friends were so drunk with this victory that all they could do was to continue the full-mouthed chant of ı Ade'. I was borne away on the shoulder-high flying ɹet of glory. But from the moment I was pulled up ɔm the girl, my feelings about the fight were hardly ɑat of gloating victoriousness. At first I took it with a kind of moral equanimity, rueful, slightly ruffled, indifference – something I should have shown before I picked up the gauntlet the girl dropped. I should have kept my phlegm in me instead of bringing it up, I shouldn't have shown willing. And who had I beaten up? A girl, ample and plump, pinpoint nipples rising through her tight uniform, a girl nevertheless. Perhaps beating up the mousiest boy in the class would have been better than tussling with the girl. I felt my victory was somewhat neutralised by its character, such a realisation of having won a dubious victory was freckled with a certain cranial airiness, gratified lightheadedness. It might as well have gone the other way. What if the girl had got the better of me and had pummelled my head to a pulp? But seeing how easy it was for me to wipe the floor – or field – with her, I doubted whether she stood any chance. And there was another reason fighting was unwise. Although Father was no longer the headmaster, if it got to him that I had fought with anyone – girl or boy – he would certainly demand an explanation and it had better be a good one. Father had been in the education system for more than two decades at the time I was leaving primary school and in all those years corporal punishment was the norm, caning being the staple of the system. Father was an adept caner, better at doing it than Mr A or any teacher or headmaster of his time. In spite of him not being a regular Bible-reader at any time in his adult life – I never saw him once read it – he believed that sparing a child the rod might not be so good for the child.

The fight is the most delineated memory I have of what may be called my first 'war' as a self-conscious person, my first serious earthly war. It was a war in so far as someone finding it in her heart to carry an act of aggression against me. A mini-war maybe, but this was how some wars started. I remember some mothers coming round to the school, livid with anger and bile, their bosoms waspishly girded, heaving and huffing, asking for the head of the boy who beat their own boy or girl up the day before. And there were cases of those who would take the fight out of school, seek out the homes of the boy who had the upper hand and set off a feud against the family. The *prima facie* trigger of the First World War, the shooting of Archduke Franz Ferdinand and his wife, has always been a byword for how a supposedly minor affair might erupt into something that would take the lives of millions of people.

At the age I was when I fought with the girl, intimations of physical conflict were all I could fully comprehend. There is another 'war', though, of which I had only a fuzzy knowledge, commonly known and acknowledged across Africa. This is the sort of war salvationist Christians might call Spiritual Battle, a war taken to a person by witches, evildoers, ill-wishers and every sort of agents of *maleficia*. When one gets to a certain age this kind of war becomes a daily threat, a continuous existential threat, a real threat, real in a suggestible, smoky way. A visit to a shaman, or a priest, or a muti-man, or a jujuman, or a marabout, or a churchman in a stripped-down Mother Hubbard costume is often no more than a confirmation of the threat or the ferocity of the insidious battle that is being waged against one. A nondescript glance from an old woman down the street is easily translated into *jettatura*, evil eye, cockatrice gaze. Tinnitus in the ear means siren calls that will induce madness if answered. Pins and needles in the arm may signify so many invisible Lilliputian arrows being sent by enemies. Headache or acouasm in the head can only be a manifestation of a ghostly mallet being smashed against the skull by unseen forces. The stone against which one stubs one's toe was certainly planted by a bogeywoman under the cimmerian cloak of the witching hour. Body-wide fibromyalgic pain and fatigue is definitely the result of voodoo, of *invultuation*, of pins being stuck into one's carven smaller simulacrum somewhere.

It was logical to expect speculations that my younger sister's illness was the result of a 'war' of some kind, and when cancer was diagnosed, it didn't come as a surprise that it was translated as an internal wound wreaked by a poison-tipped arrow shot by an enemy, or by a posse of enemies.

Three Old Women

I only knew two grandparents and they were grandmothers. Mother's father died in 1947, 20 years before I was born. All I know about him are stories Mother rehearsed to me. He was one of a handful of people who had Western education in his hometown. He worked as an interpreter and clerk in the colonial courts before he became a taxman, moving from one town to another in three colonial districts. Although she didn't follow her father from place to place, Mother seemed to know a lot about the journeys her father took in the early last century. The travelling taxman often rode in passenger trucks mostly after sundown, and there was a rare night when Mother travelled with her father. The truck broke down a few miles after they started the journey and the passengers had to footslog for hours: the villages they walked through, the birdcry and mammalian ululations, the reptilian sibilations, the cricketcry and various nocturnal cawing and cooing, the barefooted tireless servants carrying stuff on their heads, tramping through the humid night, sweating.

For some years during Mother's early life her father was absent, or sketchily present, he was busy collecting taxes and levies, doing a bit of on-the-road bookkeeping and district-round auditing of colonial accounts. And, polygamously, he had taken several women as wives. Mother lived with her mother, a trader and draper.

Although she was a shrewd businesswoman, Grandma (she will henceforth be called 'Grandma' to differentiate her from Father's mother) did not have any classroom education, so she was not thinking of sending her only daughter off to school, and Grandfather was too busy travelling around the colonial world and having a good few children by other wives. But he came round one day and asked how Grace – my mother – was getting on at primary school. He was told Mother started school but that Grandma had not been too keen on her daughter wasting precious time in education, she would prefer that she was helping her sell stuff at her stall in the town's market, preparatory to when she would own her own stall. Grandfather was livid: no child of his, however many he had, boy or girl, would not go to school. He sent for a schoolteacher younger friend of his, Mr Johnson, and entrusted the eight-year-old girl to him. Mr Johnson, an honourable family man, took it upon himself to transport the child to school on his bicycle. Mother still thanks late-lamented Mr Johnson for making it possible that she got an education. And she told me how, years later, she had taught her mother the Yoruba alphabets so that she would be able to read the Bible in the language.

Grandfather was 48 when he died in 1947. There is a murky, foxed, roach-pissed photograph of the man in the sitting room of the old house he built in the 1930s. This is the only surviving picture of the man: he wears what may have been a white coat over what looks like khaki-coloured trousers, he is balding, and the intense character of his eyes can still be picked out of the time-distressed photograph. He was 45 when the photograph was taken. Perhaps it was the cane with which he posed, he looked somewhat older than his age, slightly bent over the cane – or maybe it was the age of the belatedly framed photograph. People in vintage photographs have the knack for never looking their age, always older and, of course, greyer.

I know precious little about Father's father beyond that he was a scion of a family in which chiefs were selected in his small hometown (a home-village, if you please); I mean the sort of Yoruba chiefship which comes with all the damask-and-plush pomp and circumstance of minor royalty. He was also an artist of sorts, a recreational woodcarver, but his more humble trade was making and selling of pestle and mortar, the big-sized ones used to pound yams. Although he died just six years before I was born, I never got to see anything he made, and it was not likely that any photograph of him was ever taken, or if it was taken I have never seen it. But I know that his second or third wife – I do not know her position – was my grandmother.

A spare, fair-skinned woman who might just as well have been an archetypal battleaxe, she would have been a quintessential suffragist if she were born and lived where such women flourished, she would have been in the van of the battle against despotic andrarchy (the rule of men). And she was so independent-minded and unamenable to patriarchal authority that she had all of her four children by four different men. I remember I couldn't get my head round the fact that Father had three other maternal half-siblings. I half understood it, though, when I grew to know my grandmother. Perhaps the older attributive 'fiery' would sit better with her than the newfangled 'feisty', but I think she was a gristly twisting of both words. Even then, I later reasoned, if my grandfather could have children with several women, what should stop my grandmother from leaving one polygamous male for another? Because she was a woman: the weaker sex, the second sex, the invisible gender, obedient, dependent, subservient. Now the snag is my grandmother didn't fit any of these descriptions, she was a peppery soul in her heyday and would ruffle Socrates' calm – she would also rattle Xanthippe's spleenishness, if Socrates decided to take her, bigamously, as second wife.

It is necessary to explain the concept of 'hometown' in the Yoruba culture. One's hometown is where one's ancestors came from, running back for hundreds of years, or as long as anyone can remember. You may go to work in Lagos, Kano, Enugu or some other city or town in Nigeria, or you may have been living in London or Milan for all of 30 years, yet your 'hometown' remains your home. All through the years I was growing up, Father worked away from his small hometown. I was born in the western Nigeria town of Owo where both Father and Mother were working as teachers. Owo is only some 25 miles from his hometown of Ikaro, and in its turn Ikaro is less than a couple of strides from Ifon, Mother's hometown. If one is driving from Owo one will arrive at Ifon first before Ikaro, which is no more than ten minutes drive from Ifon town centre. And for all of the years Father worked in Owo, he went to Ikaro at least once a month, sometimes stopping over to say a brief hello to his mother-in-law in Ifon. While Father never built – he never really intended to build – any house in Owo, he had a beautiful – I'd say pretty – house in his hometown Ikaro, a half-stone, half-brick, five-room cottage. Grandmother lived in the house and she never stopped prettifying it and its environs. At the time we were going 'home' with Father, the house had been transfigured into a picturesque gateau-piece, falling just short of becoming a folly. She often had the house's tricolour paint retouched. The house was fenced in with bluntly pointy palings which she painted brilliant white, and she often spent a lot of time repairing the fence, twisting and re-twisting the wire which held the slats together. There was an orchard at the back, planted with mango trees, coconut and palm trees, cashew, orange and tangerine, and a kind of tree which bore fruits they called 'African apple'. There was a small pond dug in a corner of the orchard, it had a number of fish at a certain time and a few toads. The grounds of the house were planted with flowers, perennials, hibiscus, roses, sunflowers and others whose names I did not know. There were the resident and visitant birds: finches, thrushes, robins and others beyond my ken. Butterflies also flourished in this small wonderland, and the fugitive dragonflies, beetles and bumblebees. The house and its surround were perhaps the most beautiful spot I knew when I was growing up.

Father always took his children 'home' at least four times a year, but not all at once, and he seldom took the girls. It seemed the old man preferred boys, his sons, as travelling companions. The first son, Dupe, who is a dozen years older than me, used to go with Father to the hometown, until he was ten and went away to boarding school, only visiting occasionally during school holidays. Then Femi had begun to visit hometown with Father. Again it was Akin and me together who travelled home with Father at the same time, never one of us alone like the two boys before us.

We used to look forward to the visits. There was something salubrious about the atmosphere, something peaceful, fragrant, Edenic. Akin and I would play games in the garden, and I found the texture of the soil of hometown pleasantly strange, a kind of grainy alluvium you would normally find close to a sea. Although there is a stream a mile or so away, the town is tens of miles from the sea. But it was as if the house, or the whole small town, was built on the waterless womb of Atlantis, or smack in the matrix of the Red Sea after the 'miraculous' parting by Moses. Bees often came to visit the flower garden and orchard, and a number of times we were warned not to stray into the orchard as bees often built hives round the branch of a particular mango tree. A couple of times Akin and I had been tempted to startle bees from their hives, but we never got round to doing that. Nor did we succeed in finishing off any toads, although many stones were let fly at them. The place was conducive to what we loved doing besides play: while Akin drew and sketched just about everything around, I spent time escaping into the fantasy world of stories, tall thrilling tales. Years later, I realised it was more than a coincidence that I always went to hometown with adventure stories: R.L Stevenson and Ryder Haggard and those prototypal magic-realist stories written in Yoruba by D.O Fagunwa, and the zany, puckish, slapsticky stories by Amos Tutuola.

Snakes were also occasional visitors to the orchard and garden, and this was another reason Grandmother always tried to keep an eye on us whenever we were larking around. I saw a few of the crawlies during our visits home and one hot sun-bathed afternoon, when Grandmother had gone out to the market and Father had gone to visit friends, I climbed the short-set cashew tree in the orchard, got myself ensconced in the fork of two arterial boughs and started to read. Moments later I was lost in Fagunwa, gulping like a hungry gannet tasty morselled streams of stories about forests, sprites, pixies, fairies, centaurs, hippogriffs and monstrous talking snakes with human heads. I must have been reading for almost an hour when, as if by intuition, I glimpsed a slender brown serpent slithering towards me, its colour blending into the mottled dunnishness of the tree bark –

it was inches from me. I dropped from the branch, smack on the ground, on all fours, sprang up and sprinted like I never did before, dashed into the house and slammed the door hard, pretty much closing the door on the prelapsarian innocence with which I walked into, and explored, the orchard. I told Akin what happened and he'd found it only too hilarious. From that day I indulged most of my book-filled alone-time in the cosiness of the house and its flower-potted porch (although a tiny green snake had once been found there).

Grandmother lived in a magical world of her own too. Although she had no problem hemming her house in with trees and even having a pond made, she had no qualms about populating the orchard and garden with imaginary things. Now if I told Grandmother that a snake had sneaked on me on the cashew tree, she would have told me off for going up a tree to read. The old woman might also begin to speculate on the possibility that the snake could be the Lamia-like witch from the next street who had come to hurt her grandchild, that was why its colour blended with the tree, and why it chose cashew tree whose bark was textured like a snake skin. During one of our visits to hometown, Grandmother had had a few of the branches of two of the three mango trees in her orchard clipped off. Soon afterwards the trees were pollarded, then barked and uprooted totally because certain malign bird spirits had turned the branches into their perches, a transit camp between their nests and coven. The pond was soon filled with sand and silt because witches intended to turn the water into bloodstained ditchwater where they could bathe and disport. The toads went first because they were no longer just toads, nor were they the incarnations of any princes charming. The toads had become a group of warlocks whose croaks would lull anyone into eternal slumber. One morning when we sat with Grandmother as she prepared tea, she asked us whether we heard some witch birds cawing and twittering in the dead of the night, the constant cackling and chirruping of the birds had kept her awake. Grandmother believed these were not the small unobtrusive birds which often forgathered in the garden; these were larger evil avianthropic birds *who* were holding a witch-palaver nearby, and maybe they knew her grandchildren were home and they wanted to do harm to them (us). Were we experiencing any pain anywhere, any headache, neck pain? No, not a wrinkle of pain, we answered. Nor did we hear witches making any sort of racket. Although sometimes when I woke up, I would hear, against the background of endless whitish cricket noise, desultory birdtalk, occasional yowls of dogs and caterwauls of cats, even at the time I thought these were natural night sounds. But if Grandmother said there were witches, maybe it was true. Anyway, she told us how she read her Yoruba-language Bible, concentrating on Psalm 23, and prayed for much of the night. Normally, before she climbed on her bed to sleep, Grandmother often knelt and prayed, and she did the same first thing in the morning. We saw her doing these devotions because she had a bunk bed in her room for visiting grandchildren – from the upper bunk I always had a bird's eye view of Grandmother hunched in prayer

But then there was a grand irony to Grandmother's arbitrary accusation of others of witchery – a melodramatic irony. During one of our visits to hometown, Akin and I were idling in the front garden of Father's house when a boy leant over the palings to talk to us when Grandmother had gone out. After some pleasantries and blather, the boy blurted out that our grandmother was a witch. We were almost physically knocked back by this piece of canard (it was an untruth, we staunchly believed). Although she still simmered with quiet self-will even at 80-odd, the old woman could not be a witch, I protested in nonplussed silence. This was our grandmother. Witches don't read the Bible, Akin managed to wring something out at last. *Oh they certainly do*, the boy replied. *When you see a witch reading a big black book that looks like a bible it isn't a bible, it is an evil book slapped with the cover and look of a bible, to deceive people.* But Grandmother often kneels to pray at night, I grumbled. *Oh she is only preparing for her nightly excursions to covens.* But Grandmother often calls other people witches, she hates witches. *Well, she only does that to avoid suspicion.* When I saw that we were not getting anywhere with the boy I tried to put some juice in my verbal resource: how did the foolish boy know that my Grandmother was a witch? Because she was a 'tough woman', he replied, she always stood her ground like a man and would bring any man to heel; any woman who traversed the wishes and opinions of men like my grandmother must be a witch. Our impertinent grandmother had even antagonised his grandfather, a powerful medicineman and masquerader, my grandmother called the man a charlatan.

I could see Akin was becoming impatient with the boy, but drawing on an unsuspected reserve of sufferance, he asked him to give yet another reason he believed Grandmother was a witch because so far everything the boy was saying was hogwash. *And she has nine fingers*, the boy said. Everyone had ten fingers but Grandmother had nine, the boy stressed. The missing finger was Grandmother's initiatory contribution to the brew she partook of the first night she presented herself at the witches' coven, she had joined others in eating her thumb as well as other collops carved from humanflesh. Now I was getting angry too. This was utter nonsense. I had noticed a few years before that there was only a bald stump where there should be a thumb on Grandmother's left hand. Curious, I had asked her son, Father, what happened to the thumb. He explained: Grandmother had lost the digit when she was a girl, she was chopping rabbit meat in her parents' farmhouse when she accidentally lopped off her finger. I told the boy this, but he laughed: *What a fine story!* But we sleep in Grandmother's room and she is always there during the night. *No, she isn't, you only see her body there, her spirit is gone – to the coven.* And the awful boy pressed on: *Your grandmother moved from one man to another when she was young because she was always shown up to be a witch.* At this point I had become as angry as Akin and clearly we could not take it anymore. By a kind of witchlike telepathy, we decided to beat the boy up, but the urchin, whose grandfather might have immersed in gris-gris to sharpen his instincts, made good of his escape as we dashed towards the gate of the fence. The rascal hollered as he hared off: *Your grandmother is a witch and if she comes to kill me, my grandfather will wake me up and then kill her!*

We decided not to tell Grandmother anything. We did not know how she would take it; although we were pretty certain she would not just stay silent and get on with whatever she was doing. The parents or grandmothers of the boy would certainly have to do a lot of explaining to avoid a thoroughgoing keelhauling. That night I spent a lot of time wondering: is Grandmother a witch? The wiry lioness and progenitrix was so good and generous to us her grandchildren that she would go out of her way to treat us to yam-with-fried-egg and Lipton tea on most mornings. Thanks to her children, tea was one exotic luxury Grandmother never deprived herself of. Although we had seen her tough-woman side a few times, she would not say a word of reproach to us her grandchildren. And she still prayed every night and morning. In popular, and often juvenile, imagination, witches normally morphed into birds, but the only bird in whose guise I could see my grandmother was that of a protective domestic mother hen, a mutant matriarchal hen larger and stronger than any bird of prey.

Along the lines of protectiveness, Grandmother did something unforgettable one midmorning. A narrow dirt-road wound through the front of the house, the road led nowhere because the street was a cul-de-sac and at the time we used to go to hometown, apart from Father's car no vehicle would be seen on the road for a whole day. There might be an occasional clapped-out bicycle or motorcycle, or persons, countable, mostly on their way to or from their farms, those one might describe as 9-5 farmers. It was clear no one had a car in the street, but once in a while vehicles would come into the street for one reason or the other. With Grandmother's approval, Akin and I sometimes took advantage of the agrarian placidity of the road to sprint competitively or kick football to each other on it, especially when Grandmother was sitting in the porch, watching. She was relaxed in her armchair that morning in the porch, keeping an eye on us, when a car came into the street from the highway and bore down on us at lethal speed. Akin grabbed hold of me and we leapt off the road in a body.

Grandmother jumped from where she sat, lifted herself spryly and we all watched the car as it streaked up the one-way street raising a spray of sand in its wake. Grandmother's eyes showed anger in the way I had never seen before, her age-lined brow became closer-grained, gathering into a glower. 'The bastard wanted to kill my grandchildren,' she hissed. We were still wondering what she would do when she shuffled down the short steps from the porch, and as she went down she called Akin to fetch her kitchen stool, a low-slung wooden seat.

Grandmother took the stool from Akin, set it plonk in the middle of the road and lowered herself onto it. We watched from the porch as Grandmother sat tight for almost two hours. After what we thought was an eternity, the croupy cascading sound of a car engine suddenly torqued itself through my ears. We raced down the porch steps and saw what was coming: a Lincoln-green VW Beetle. It was clear the Afro-haired driver was gearing up for a speed-surge when he was surprised by an old woman sitting in the middle of the road. He honked his horn many times, choppily. Grandmother ignored the young man. So with supercilious impatience he pressed the horn again, now at length, going at it for about two minutes nonstop. When he saw this availed nothing, he put his head out of the window and shouted:

'Old woman, clear off the road, or you're dead. I will run you over.'

Grandmother remained silent. She didn't budge.

'Hey, bugger off, old woman. You're wasting my time. I am a salesman. Time is money, mad old woman.'

Now Grandmother raised her voice:

'It is your grandmother who is mad, your great-grandmother. You nearly killed my grandchildren and you have the effrontery to disrespect me. You lack breeding, young man, and I will teach you how to behave to those older than you.'

Then like a kind of anthropomorphic goddess who had appeared to spurn a fallen, recalcitrant worshipper, Grandmother turned her back to the car and its occupant.

Frustrated, the young man put the car in reverse and the crudely-engineered creature growled round a small bend in the road like an antlion larva backing itself out of its sandpit. Grandmother remained where she was, unperturbed, inscrutable, aware that there was no way the car could leave the street without going through where she sat.

The car reappeared a few minutes later and now there was someone in the 'shotgun' seat. It was a gentleman, late-fiftyish, who had fallen on hard times in Lagos years before and had come back to hometown to live in a house he built far up the street when he was somewhat in the money – and when he had a car; now he lived in spare superannuation. He came out of the VW Beetle with the young driver and without hesitation they went round the stool on which Grandmother sat. And as if to confirm the old woman's godhood, immediately the men prostrated themselves at her foot. Shooting neither from the hip nor from the shoulder, the tone of his voice excessively conciliatory, the older man spoke:

'Mama, I have reprimanded this fool. He told me you are upset because he sped through this road.'

Grandmother clarified: 'And he nearly killed my grandchildren. Then he called me a mad woman.'

'Oh God', the man said, apparently appalled. 'Speak up, you fool, speak up and apologise to Mama.'

The young driver slightly sneaked out his diminishing Afroed head out of the vulnerable carapace of his dashiki and said: 'I am sorry, Mama. Pardon me, Mama. I beg you, Mama.'

Avoiding any eye contact with the withered-up driver of the VW Beetle, Grandmother rose, picked up her stool and gave a dismissive gesture indicating that the young man could go. But as she made towards her house, the older man said in a subdued all but genuflective voice: 'Bless him, bless the idiot, Mama, so he will arrive safely where he is going. He has offended you a lot, Mama. He has put a curse on his own head when he insulted your grey hair.'

'He will arrive safely.'

The house was built on Howlett Street, and years later when Grandmother had died at about the age of 95, outliving her son, Father, by a year I composed an eclogue – *Blacked Sepulchre* – whilst home on holiday with Mum who was now living in the house.

At the start of Howlett Street a start of an equatorial
rain refuges me under the first shelter I see.
Briefly I crave the soul of the rain-doctor,
I crave the power to send the rain back to its blind
tyrannical sender: piss yourself if you want, Lord
of the Skies (no, I am not playing on words: not Lord
of the Flies – *Lord of the Skies),*
but do not let it drip and drop on me.
I imagine the heavensbound Tyrant getting
pissed off now and sending his thunder to strike sense
into me, shock me into reverence, or combust me
into the infernal counterpart of his calmer kingdom.
But somehow I feel I am in a Faraday Cage here,
shielded from the treachery of the sky Tyrant.
Well really, this shed-like lookum that observes
the roadway is Mr Howlett's sepulchre, off-whited.
Arthur Howlett, as long dead as 1906 at age 26,
a watery death like any of the fish he'd gone to
fly-fish – so his crutched epigraph says, reared like
hung headstone on the breast of the sepulchre.
At the foot of the grave I stand safe from rain,
wondering whether bits of the lowgrown hardies on
the gravebed are Mr Howlett's fingers, or his hair,
recalling Mr Hardy's surmise, and like groomed hair
the plants are cut low and cropped, the blossoms
barbered to modest effect. I wonder as I have
wondered a thousand times:
what does Mr Howlett look like?
Tall, thin, oh certainly stringy. (The sun and sweat
often squeezed lard out of fat colonials.)
I am certain he is now brown, toasted by the sun,
his brains convectioning under the topee, boiling,

broiling, a bagful of atlases burdening his back...
Then Mr Howlett appears, truly browned, burnt,
blotched hands tugging at his auburn
boyish beard, tall and straight...
And nothing burdens his back, he stands, arms
kimboed like a human headstone to his grave,
topee-less, tousle-haired, khaki shorts and shirt
slightly stained and lightly starched with earth...
and cracked short-socked brogues,

'Good day, young man,' the young Briton says.
'Hello,' I reply, checking myself from
retorting about 'A young man calling
another young man young man.'
'I am Arthur Howlett. I died 86 years ago
and was buried here.'
'I do know that. But I do not believe this is you,
I do not believe in ghosts. I am a rationalist.'
'Well, I don't know whether I am a ghost or not, but this is me, Arthur Howlett. And be careful about too much rationalism, young man,
sometimes things are not as
they seem.'
'So maybe you are a merely a travelling illusionist
from England, trying to make me believe you are
Arthur Howlett.'
'I am who I say I am, young man.'
'And will you stop calling me "Young Man",
you look hardly older than me, Mr Howlett.'
'All right, may I call you Mr Oriku?'
'Ade. Not your "Ade" from Adrian.
Frenchify it: Adé. Or shall I say Yoruba-ise it.'
'Call me Art – from Arthur'
'Art, then. You were 26 and you still look
26, anyway.'
'That is the privilege that death brings with it,

you cease to age.'
'Oh, what a thought.'
'And Mr Rationalist. Not everything—'
'Do not be sarcastic, Arthur. Mr Howlett.'
'I am not. I only wanted to ask whether you believe in the existence of soul.'
'Well, if I can talk to someone who died almost a century ago, maybe there is such a thing as soul.'
'All right there is soul, what speaks to you now is my soul. 'Even though I can see you? In the flesh?'
'Well, it's more complicated than what I can begin to explain now.'
'So your soul is still here, shouldn't it to have returned to London or Liverpool or wherever you came from?'
'I can visit all those places anytime I want. I am a free soul. But here is my place.'
'Here in this grave?'
'In this grave, in this village, in the whole place. I am grounded here. When I died, your grandmother was ten. I could see her crying, sobbing for the "white man". Grown older, she took it upon herself to be the custodian of this grave.
I blessed her for this, I gave her a gift, the gift of tea. Haven't you stopped and wonder why your grandmother loved tea more than anyone in the town? That was as
much as I could confer as an Englishman: tea-drinking gift.
I've run into her in the soulworld a couple of times, I see your father too and your sister who came to the other side in 1986, just a couple of years older than I was in 1906.
They all send their love.'
'And what about your folks in England, don't you see any of them at what you call the other side?'

'I do see them too, my father, mother. I was an only child. It broke their hearts when I died.'
'And why weren't you taken to England?'
'There was no point doing that. It would only
break my parents' hearts more. Anyway we are
reunited now...
Now—'
A flash of lightning and a clap of thunder slap me
back, pull me up from falling deeper
into the rich tub of goo.

The rain has ceased, merely a serein now,
and somehow it's all calm and serene,
and I remember
the myth we believed as children, of the passing
angel, when all in a classroom fell silent, all at once.

Mother's mother lived on the other side of town. In many ways she was different from Father's mother. Although they were just about the same age, Grandma was fuller, more matronly than Grandmother, she was the quintessential earth mother. In a kind of healthy rivalry between in-laws, Grandma complained to both Mother and Father that she often did not 'see' much of us, her grandchildren, that the other grandmother was having the best of time with us, that Dad only stopped briefly on his way to his hometown and mother. She wanted us to spend time with her too, maybe a week or two. She was also very keen on feeding Akin and me up because she thought we were too thin, even underfed, so much so that when she looked at us the only thing she could discern was a melded apparition of two malnourished little boys. Mother told her to no avail that she was pretty much overfeeding us, and that it was not likely that her mum would be able to make roly-poly Tweedledee and Tweedledum of us as she wished. The old woman knew nothing about the possibility of 'thin' or 'fat' genes, there was only one thing on her mind: engorging us unto *embonpoint*.

While she offered no reason for Akin's thin physique, Grandma's explication of my own leanness was Shakespearean and sage in its plangency. During her visits to Owo in my preteen years, bookless Grandma was desperately confounded that I was always reading one book or the other, and that even if the TV was on I'd ignore it, riveted by a book. Of course, these were adventure stories and getting lost in them was far more delectable than watching the best of Baba Sala sitcoms – which I also loved. Grandma would admonish: 'go out and play with your peers, little boy. Keeping your nose in a book every time is not good. No wonder you are skinny – the food you should have used to fatten up is wasted on reading.' Years later, I realised Grandma might not be too wide of the mark. Reading of books, or to use the appropriate phrase, eating of books – bibliophagy – might indeed have resulted in my wispiness, after all whatever one reads in a book metabolises in the brain, reading only nourishes the mind, not the body, and who knows how much calories one burns when one reads? And the old woman's diagnosis easily recalls Shakespeare's Caesar who hazarded that Cassius' progressive lankiness had been the symptom of too much thinking? In a way, like Cassius, I was hypercerebrating, which was why I macerated. By the way, how would a book look in the hand of Sir John Falstaff?

We looked forward to spending time with Grandma to vary the routine of the other grandmother's candied grotto and the Wordsworthian lyricality of the milieu. Grandma's abode was diametrically different. She lived among her extended family in a house built in period peristylar fashion with two large courtyards adjoining each other. Each yard had twelve rooms and in the eight corners of the yards were large barrel-shaped earthenpots, catchments for rainwater that everyone shared. The mortared adobe sprawl was built by Grandma's father, a well-off man who had several wives and many children. The rooms were occupied by relatives and a number of tenants, the yards teemed with people: parents, children and the elderly. There was a large kitchen in the back of the house, often choked with woodsmoke, although only a fraction of those who lived in the house cooked in the kitchen, most of the residents used kerosene cookers in front of their rooms, just under the timber-colonnaded eaves of the roofs of the yards. In the evenings, sounds of assegai-long pestles being pounded against bole-cut mortars melded into the chafing sound of many manual grindstones crunched against each other. These sounds blended into the atonal carilloned clatter coming from many spots where children were washing up enamelled steel plates and stainless steel spoons. The courtyards were quite a sight when families were cooking their supper, it was an anthill of gastrofrenzy, a ready metaphor for cooking up a storm. And the smell – the aroma of a *salmagundi* of stews, soups and savouries. A platoon of women, girding their bosoms with their wrappers, would be busy at work. These women and their daughters often helped older women – like Grandma – in the compound. There was a deep well in the backyard, forbidden to children and beyond it was an area of bush about half an acre, an undeveloped plot of land belonging to the late patriarch. The sooty beams of the kitchen roof were hung with husked corns and millets, fumed by the smoke and steam in the kitchen.

One evening when we stopped over with Father, about a dozen children were sitting in a wide circle in one of the courtyards, swapping stories, their faces lustrously bloomed by the silvery talc of the moon. The boon of electricity, which reached the town only a few years before, was yet to be extended to the house. And we could see many pigeons flapping, shuffling, billing and cooing in the courtyards.

Our wish to spend some time with Grandma was granted when, in the middle of the long school vacation, Father drove into town, then straight to his mother-in-law's place, got our bags out of the car boot and told us we were to spent one full week with the old woman before he would come round to pick us up again. We were quietly elated.

Grandma told us that though we could play as long as we wanted in and around the house, we must not wander too far, and must not go near the well. She did not say anything about the bush in the back, which we had imagined might be worth peering into – although the bush might be close to the town centre, any number of Fagunwa's fairy sylvans might be found there, I imagined. And the old woman tried as best as she could to feed us, practically force-feed us, admonishing us for nibbling rather than eating. She was daily disappointed that the hillocks of *eba* and *iyan* and substantially fricasseed stews, cornucopian pottages and ragouts, she placed before us were more than two-thirds unfinished. It appeared she took her desire that we bloat and fill out before we leave rather too seriously. If given the choice the old woman would have loved to dollop up the stodge she placed before us and cram it down our throats in the same way one might drench orphaned cubs. An active Anglican senior churchwoman, Grandma read the Yoruba Bible and prayed every night and morning – seeing the way she was concerned about fattening us up,

I wondered whether she might have asked God, in her prayers, to slap more of his creational clod on us.

On the second day, we were told that there was a witch among the people who lived in the house. Naturally the witch was an old woman, older than Grandma, exceedingly wizened, grizzled and ancient. Although we did not make a lot of friends among the children in the house, a boy of about our age had told us how everyone had taken the woman as a witch. Although Akin and I never discussed the nasty boy who called our Father's mother a witch a few months before, there would have been mutual relief that this other boy, who had flaky patches of ringworm on his head, did not say Grandma was a witch – nevertheless, he brought up a brief and dauntingly vivid déjà vu in me. He began with when his mother lost one of her children, his baby sister, and had told some of those who came to commiserate with her that the old woman had hexed her daughter and had killed her, and might have skewered and spit-roasted the baby's muttony flesh during a witch-fest. With an inquisitorial skill I seemed to have acquired with the first boy, I asked the ringworm-headed one how his mother knew the old woman killed her daughter, he replied that his mother knew because the old woman was a witch. Then I asked the boy how his mother knew a baby tasted like mutton, he couldn't quite remember whether his mother actually said anything about the baby being skewered and barbecued, but he insisted that everyone knew that to witches' strange collective palate, a baby tasted like mutton, roast mutton. He told us that no one shared the rainwater in the vat in front of her room with her and that the old woman's witch spirit, or soul, was buried deep in one of the pigeons she bred. The bush behind the house was where she had sabbats with other witches.

The old woman lived alone in the farthest corner of the second courtyard, her room was almost right-angled against the corner – or not quite, it was tweaked slightly to the south of the courtyard, a door to the backyard opening up beside to the left. A very old woman, overwhelmingly puckered-up, blind in one eye with the lids firmly shut, and the white of the other eye was so red that it set off the brown nucleus into a fiery girandole. The lashes around the good eye were starkly traced with kohl, further giving the eye a kind a cyclopean appearance. The old woman always tied her wrapper round her waist, her shrivelled breasts, dugs, dangling or lying pat on her almost fleshless ribcage. The most striking thing we saw in the old woman was her hands and forearms: up to the elbow the arms were deep-coloured, staringly dark-pigented like ink on litmus paper. The old woman was a weaver of cloth, she worked with dye, and for stretches of time she would sit at the loom under the eaves. The loom was placed against the wall and never-opened window of her room. We watched the old woman weave cloth with some interest. At the loom the crone seemed to be working wonders – *Clotho fiddling her distaff against spindle threads.* The cloth on the loom was of several shades of blue, from inky to hyacinthine, as characterless as the one she tied, but the way her hands worked, her fingers, they were like fingers working the strings of a harp, or a zither. I think Akin and I tacitly agreed with each other that this woman truly looked like a witch – or what we imagined a witch looked like. And subtly we began what I can only describe as a witch-hunt. Or, broadly speaking, witchcraft investigation.

When we went beyond the woodsmoked kitchen into the bush behind the house, we followed a path that led to a grove. The grove was planted with a number of broad-leaved plantains and bananas, with cocoyams, palmettos and a stunted guava. In the bowery shade, a number of earthenpots were scatteredly rooted in the soil. We peered into the vats and saw that every one of them was filled with blue-black liquid, like peaty putrid blood – witch-brew. Spooked, we fled back into the house, but later that day we discovered what the pots were for. The old woman used them to dye the cloths she wove. Stealthily, we followed her as she went into the grove and watched through the self-trellised vegetation to see her dip her knaggy hands into one of the kiers. Using her arm as a swizzle stick she made motions of mixing something up in the pot and after a while she brought out whorls of threaded bice-blue cotton. She didn't see us watching, but we were chased back into the house by the stench of fermenting woad.

The old woman spent some time in the grove. But after a while we got curious again and toddled out to see whether the old crone had transmogrified into a crow or vulture, whether she had turned cooking-pots into dyepots or had been joined by a dozen other witches, a gloomy circle of chatoyant-eyed soucouyants all taking on odd shapes, celebrating their own kind of Childermas with mock-turtle soup in which the heads of babies had replaced calves' heads – well, mock-calf soup. Before we even entered the bush we found the woman in the swept clearing between the kitchen and bush. *Like Lachesis, the middle sister of the Fates,* the old woman was measuring out yarns of just a couple of shades of blue, and she was so taken with this that she did not notice us even though we jumped when we saw her.

When next we saw the boy, we asked him to expand on what he knew about the old woman's witchery. All right, she caused the death of his baby sister, so what else had she done? He told us about a tortoise who lived with the old woman in her room. The tortoise seldom came out of the dark place, and if it came out it would only crawl around in front of her room, never stepping over the invisible line between what was considered the old woman's space and others'. The shy tortoise would return to the old woman's room, not to be seen for weeks. The boy said that imprisoned in the tortoise's carapace were the trapped spirits of those whose deaths she had machinated, her two husbands who died young, the one child she had, and many others. The tortoise was said to have been as long-living as the woman, maybe a 100 years. I pretty much gave this credence, thanks to Aesop and several stories about *the* tortoise in the early-primary Yoruba storybook, in which the tortoise is given the power of speech, wisdom, cunning and canniness, dressed up, shoed and capped. We never saw the old woman's tortoise in the days we stayed in the compound, though.

The boy also told us about a girl who came to live with the old woman a couple of years before. The girl looked strange: bald head, spindly limbs, big belly, bulging rheumy eyes, sweating palms, flared runny nose. She was believed to have been a witch in her own right, or actually the old woman may have 'given' her witchery. She was an orphan, the old woman's great-grandniece by some removals. And the girl was sickly often. Although she barely ate, she had constant constipation pains. No one knew what was wrong with the girl. The old woman, part herbalist, decocted herbs and pieces of tree bark she plucked and scraped from the bush in an earthenpot and fed it to the girl every day. It did not work. One day someone found the girl, close to the arboretum where the woman had her big dyepots, she was using her hands to scoop up sandy soil and eating it. The girl suffered from pica, the urge to eat things that should not be eaten. She was what I later realised in adulthood might be called a *geophage*, earth-eater, she fed on soil as if it was a kind of earthly manna. And who would do such a thing if not a little girl tortured by witchery? One day the girl was taken away, never to return. Soon the news came that she had died.

Then the boy repeated how the old woman's soul resided in one of her pigeons. The old woman bred several of the birds and they lived in four earthenpots tucked closely against the front of her room, the other side of the loom. Except for one, all of the pigeons were white, although there was now dirt-made depth to the white. The pigeons pottered around the courtyards, often not straying far from the inner courtyard where the old woman lived. There was a dog in the compound that worried the pigeons, sometimes closing on them while the old woman was looking. An afternoon that the dog growled and snapped at the pigeons was the only time I heard the old woman say anything. She snorted at the dog to leave her birds alone, calling on the 'master' of the dog, who, obviously, was not within hearing, to keep it on a leash. Whenever the dog snapped or growled or charged at the pigeons they would flap, lift themselves for seconds, bank and scurry into their minuscule caves. The birds could not fly, they might be called 'homing pigeons' in so far as they knew how to home in on their earthencotes to escape the dog. But sometimes, not seeing the dog for a length of time, the pigeons would wander from their hole-against-the-wall snuggery, out to the back of the house. They liked to play in the ground between the kitchen and the bush, rootling through the soil for ants, often carrying back into the house dry stripped snapped tines of palm fronds. Bunches of these tines were used as brooms, and as old as she was the woman always swept clean the clearing behind the kitchen. The pigeons were taking pieces of broken broom-fibre from the clearing and anywhere else they could find them, into their potholes. To make the straw-beds *they* – the pigeons – would sleep on, the boy told us. And there was the old woman's special pigeon, the only grey one among the whites, actually shades of greys prettily spotted with white. The pigeon was different, robuster than all, she had a roost to herself, she was like the queen, a queen pigeon if there was anything like that, a queen to whom others were drones, workers and mere courtiers. And she must have been aware of her specialness: she didn't often move with the others, her plumes, though darker, were cleaner, radiant, and when she preened and ruffled her feathers she revealed an alluring symmetry of nimbus-grey and moon-white, easy on the eye. It was in the bird that the witch soul of the old woman reposed. And although the pigeon might look beautiful now, at night when it needed to attend a coven, it would take on another shape and feature: uglier, beakier, altogether vulturine.

So if the bird was killed the soul of the woman would die? I asked this singular question, half-declaratively, but none of us could provide an answer to it. But any child who had heard about witches would also have heard the tale of the witch who, in the shape of a crow, was winging her way towards a witch conclave and, unfortunately, flew past the open window of a jujuman whose sortilegious prowess was extraordinary. The jujuman sent a poisoned arrow after the witch – an anti-Cupid sort of arrow – and hit her. The witch dropped from the sky, seriously wounded and maimed. In another town 30 miles away, a middle-aged woman suddenly began to sicken with pain in her chest, mimicking the spot where the witch-bird had been hit by the arrow – the gullet. Even stigmata-like blood began to trickle from a spot on the woman's breast. And as the bird died where it fell, the woman also died in her room that very night, after she had confessed to her witchery and the fact that she was the doppelganger of the bird who'd just been silenced. So, to some extent, we knew what it meant to kill the 'soul' of a witch.

No one said anything again about witches and their souls until a day before Father would come to pick us up. The boy had cornered us in one of the courtyards and had shown us two Y-shaped catapults. He said he was an adroit sharp-shooting catapulter, and that his hunting ground was the clearing behind the kitchen where the old woman always hung her yarns to dry before weaving them. Sometimes the place was visited by lizards, geckos, an occasional rodent and small rabbit, mostly visitors from the bush. Once in a while he would go into the bush, hoping to pot a bird or two. He'd killed a number of lizards, geckos and a mouse. What he would love to kill was a bird but they were proving rather tricky to get. He invited us for a hunt, we could look if there was any lizard in the rear of the kitchen and if there was nothing, we might go into the bush and try bringing down a bird or two. This was an interesting proposition.

Although I had not seen Alfred Hitchcock's *Birds* at the time – frankly, I had never been to a cinema – that night I dreamt of an army of grey pigeons, the domestic birds had now taken on a hawk-like look, wantonly-taloned, with beaks so sharp and hooked that they would unpick one's entrails in minutes. The huge pigeons were winging hard after me while I raced through a desolate footpath, sealed on both sides with gnarled, close-grained pleaching of vegetation. The grotesque pigeons flapped their heavy dark wings, screeched, spat warm globby spit and shat dense gobby birdshit on me. I ran for dear life, screaming without sound. I saw a house, a monstrous Kafkaesque castle, the door was ajar. I barged in. I seemed to have entered a convent of the Sisters of Darkness. And who did I find sitting regally at the head of an ancient refectory table? The old woman was

Mother Superior here, her eye now deeply and singularly igneous, rutilant, reptilian, and at the table with her were some ten or so old crones, they were feasting on a spread of something I could not pick up in the dream. Mock-calf soup, maybe. Horrified, I woke up.

Akin and I had never held a rubber catapult, to say nothing of shooting it, but after the boy had suggested that we hunt with him, we both expressed the desire to kill a lizard, although a bird would be a prize kill, maybe with our help the boy would achieve his goal now. We set out for the gravid ground-beyond-the-kitchen, the killing ground. And despite the chatter we were engaged in as we entered the ground from the courtyard, the old woman, surprising herself on us again, had not taken any notice. I wondered briefly, as we dashed back into the courtyard, whether she was half-deaf, just as she was half-blind. And as we speedily retraced our steps into the courtyard the picture of what the old woman was doing flicked in and out of my mind: with her steel-blue hand she held a knife to a dried strip of indigo yarn, slung around the line ouroboros-shaped, cutting the threads slowly but surely. *Atropos with her Damoclean knife – a merciless misericorde.*

A few hours later, in the afternoon, we met up with the boy again. The old woman was now weaving at the loom. We passed her as we bustled to the back of the kitchen, the veritable hunting ground. And what did we find when we got there? Birds, the pigeons, all ten of them. We saw the dust-streaked white ones first, they were cooingly pecking for ants in the soil with their tiny beaks and claws. Startled, they made a kerfuffle and swiftly processed into the courtyard. And that was when the boy saw the grey pigeon, the one in whose body the old woman's soul was supposedly ensconced. Apparently oblivious of our presence, its rump in the air, the bird continued to forage for snack in the sand. I did not know when the boy set a little stone in his catapult, but I heard the whizz and snap and caught sight of the stone as it hit the small head of the pigeon. It seemed the bird was too stunned to struggle to hold on to life. She flapped her wings briefly, flicked her head, looped her neck tortuously, like a poult convulsed fatally by a kind of tarantism, and flopped. Silence. Flustered and scared, we all trotted into the courtyard, not glancing at where the old woman sat weaving. The boy disappeared into his parents' bedsitter and Akin and I retreated into Grandma's rooms, sitting tight for a few hours before it was bedtime.

Early the next morning Father arrived to pick us up. We left without knowing how the old woman took the killing of her bird. When we went to hometown again with Father months later, the old woman had been dead for many weeks, apparently around the time the boy took aim at her pigeon, maybe a few days after the death of her bird, her supposed familiar. We overheard Grandma telling Father how kind-hearted and generous the old woman was, how she was never poisoned by her inability to bear children, calmly accepting that some people would blame her for this, viciously call her 'barren'. She liked children nevertheless, she took care of them, gave them food and even money, but she became sad and started to keep to herself when some children in the house began to sneak into her room when she wasn't there and stealing her money…

A Death in the Family

At 19 I knew well enough the explicit meaning of death and few of its wordy euphemisms like 'the supreme price' or 'nature's debt', and the fact that it was one hell of a disappearing act. But naturally, up till that moment, whatever books I might have read – philosophy, essays, poetry, even if I were precociously poetic and worldly-wise like Arthur Rimbaud and had tied up all of my literary work at 16 – there would still be a clockwork dimension to the way I thought about something like death, at least as far as my immediate family was concerned. The mechanistic schema would go like this: any living grandparent should go first; then parents, and not after having lived to ripe old ages like their own parents. There should be a triage of passage. It would not have mattered that one might have lost a classmate or even a friend, one's sister who was 28 was not supposed to die. But when such a thing happened there was bound to be a frenzied shuffling, by an invisible hand, of the card-deck of reality, the ace that one imagined one held becoming, magically, a joker, mocking and laughing and the glint in its eyes, the spin of its pirouette, betraying mischief. My sister's death in 1986 hit everyone in the family hard and for me it was a fontal experience, it marked the beginning of my growth into a thinking adult, the start of the unending process of maturation.

Just as the 1980s began, Mother's mother had come to live with us. She was now 85, give or take a couple of years. No one knew her exact age, but her husband, the tax officer, made an educated approximation after they met. Grandma had come to stay with us five years before, when she was ill and had to be admitted to hospital. Mother was her only daughter and although the old woman did not want to be a burden on her two children, in a system in which only the family can offer reasonable welfare or what is called 'social security' in other climes, the old woman had no choice but to accept the ministrations of her daughter. After she left hospital in 1976, Grandma stayed with us for a few months. When Father brought her from Ifon in 1981 she was as ill as before, but now she refused to be taken to a hospital. She said it was unnecessary. From the first day she came, she expressed the wish to be taken away as soon as possible. More than the suffering, she did not wish to be a burden on her daughter's family. But Grandma would stay with us for another six months, gently and untemporisingly cruising through the twilight, through that characterless realm of *Thanatopia*.

Mojisola, my big sister, who came two years before the Independence Baby, Folake, was a teacher in Owo, and lived in another neighbourhood. At the time Grandma came to live with us, she was with baby, a few months gone, and in inverse proportion, just as her pregnancy grew, Grandma's geriatric health continued to fail, a resonant case of crescendo and diminuendo slide-ruling against each other. Of course, as old as Grandma was, no one was looking forward to her death. She was a good woman, I never heard her raise her voice, and whenever she came round to visit, she always gave her younger grandchildren more than enough pin-money every day to buy snacks. A woman fried and sold tasty crunchy ripe plantain crisps down the street, and whenever Grandma came to visit, she always kept me flush enough with pennies to guttle on crisps every day. Even today there is a gastronomic association of Grandma with any food that crunches and has sherbety flavour. I do not doubt Grandma's intention in giving us money, actually she did not even know nor try to suggest what the money would be spent on, it might just as well be used to buy a paper kite, a ping-pong ball, or bubble gum. But seeing how Grandma seemed to be very concerned about Akin and me gaining more flesh, unconsciously she might be hoping that we would spend the money on things like plantain crisps, *goujons*, roast corn, or fried bean-paste, eatable things that might contribute to our fattening. Although even if she was well, by 1981 Grandma would have accepted that her two younger grandchildren might not acquire puppy fat even in puberty – middle-age girth and chops maybe, but then she would be long gone then. Now in her last days, what concentrated her mind as she slipped away was the well-being of her granddaughter, Mojisola, who was in the final stages of her pregnancy. In the last few weeks of her life, the only question she wanted an answer to was how Mojisola was doing. And by the time my sister fell into labour, Grandma had reached borderland, she was delicately balanced on the sill of oblivion, barely conscious. And for Mojisola, it was not so much a difficult labour as a difficult birth. The snooze-easy transition Grandma was going through poignantly jarred with the birth throes my sister experienced. Although, again, at the age I was I could take the full measure of how the very act of birthing could be touch-and-go, how what was supposed to be a prelude to joy could easily end in tears, sometimes unalleviated tears if the content of the pregnancy itself and the principal did not survive the strain. Big Sister's condition was cliffy, the afterpains were long, difficult and complicated. She needed blood. I remember my brother, Femi, a freshman in a technical college then, giving blood gladly, and rallying his college friends, lining them up, in case Big Sister needed more. Mother and Father were anxious, Mother more than all, for her own mother seemed ready to embrace quietus. And if we the grandchildren could look at the old woman with heart-warming summery solemnity, with fondness, how would Mother have felt? Again during the months that I was seduced by the Muse, this family Passion Week inspired the poem that I called *Morning*.

Only a shadow remains, well-thinned by twilight.
She sickens for nothing but that the malaise of night
has come – approaching swiftly: night, the jangly
toll of timeless night. Lost in the vagaries of the moon,
with the mists of her memory are her years,
even Mother knows them not, but Mother does it all,
dresses her, feeds her, sits her, cradles her, cleans
her.

Wonder!
How I wonder, this is the mother of Mother,
she is no newborn like the one Big Sister is
bringing forth. So between mother and daughter
Mother shares her cares,
between hospital and home she pares her paces.

Evening.
Mother leaves mother for daughter,
tells us to keep an eye on Old Mother.
Evening deepens,
Brother reminds us to see how Mother's
mother lies – in fragile disarray, we see. Range her
well we do try, but upon her unquestioning frame
we meet still, upon her creased flesh we feel chill,

upon her breast me meet silence, cooled-off stillness.
Desperate, we seek the wrist – we meet yet again still,
stilled pulse, chilled alabaster brow and an
undertinge of livor.

The candle bedside has burnt low, guttered and
snuffed. Unspooked, we stumbled to light
a light but Father happens in
with torchlit light, glances at Mother's mother once
and again, then sagely, he says: she's gone to sleep
for her night has come. It's late in the night too,
children, go to sleep, go to bed, it is late, it is night,
morning will soon be round.

Morning.
Morning sees Mother in all smiles and tears
and between these, she says: Old Mother, my mother,
your grandmother has now become your sister's
daughter, my daughter's daughter.

Mojisola's baby was called Yejide: *Old Mother, Grandmother, has returned*, or appropriately, *Old Mother has reawakened, risen, again*. Although no one knew the moment Grandma breathed her last, it was assumed that Yejide was born just about the time. Mother must have been thrown hither-thither by a tidal wave of passions, yo-yoing from passion-pain to passion-joy, consumed by a uterine play of emotions, she was the link in the human chain, the motivity, the crucial mitochondrion within the continuum of life. Grandma was given a respectable burial. She was taken to her hometown and, being a keenly observant Christian, was laid to rest in the churchyard of St Paul's Anglican Church.

Yejide, a sweet child, was more than any family would ask for as replacement. And when her mum returned to college to gain more qualifications in her teaching career, she stayed with her grandma, Mother. Mojisola went some hundreds of miles away to a college in the northern part of Nigeria. She always came home during holidays, and I can remember now how we would all sit together telling her stories about how Yejide was getting on. In her final year at college, Big Sister wrote to our parents to announce that she had now become a born-again Christian. She was the first person to go evangelical in our family. There seemed to have been an established Anglican religious tradition within the family. Both of the grandmothers were Anglican, Grandma was even an Elder in St Paul, Ifon, she was what was called Mother of the Church in the same way the British Parliament has Father of the House. Mother was a senior member of Mother's Union in the Cathedral of Owo, she was very active in the church, a member of YWCA, Women's Guild, and was a synodist. In 1984, Mother was part of the celebration float of the 140th anniversary of Anglicanism in Nigeria, a colourful week-long commemoration of the arrival of Christian Missionary Society on the shores of Yorubaland. Africanised Dutch print that told the story-so-far in dates and Warholian reduplication, was commissioned and worn by many congregants in the cathedral. Mother sometimes looked back at when she used to attend church with Father many years before, but by the time I grew to know that people went to church on Sundays, Father had long stopped attending. He was an Anglican only in principle, I never saw him pray, nor did I see him appeal to God by rote like a lot of people around, or indulge in any kind of devotions, but I knew he would still describe himself as a Christian, an Anglican, and he was a member of the

Synod until his death in 1990, so he'd remained a lifelong lay member of the church.

Besides a collection of the works of Jim Reeves, records full of songs that I found incredibly tedious and grave as a child, there were these two LP albums, bought in the 1970s, which harked back to Father's probably temperate taste in classical Christian music. A double vinyl record of Christmas carols, made in a cathedral in England, and Handel's *Messiah*. The carol album jacket was illustrated with arched stained-glass windows that had colourful *trompe l'oeil* patterns. Although I recognised the familiar strains of the carols on the radiogram, *Messiah* was another matter: it meant absolutely nothing to me. Despite the constant reprise of *Hallelujah* in one of the tracks, to me most of the music in the album sounded strange and eerie, plaintive string sounds, echoic asexual timbres and basilican acoustics fairly flattened by the grooves in the vinyl. The illustration on the album sleeve was characterised by Judaeo-Christian images, massed and detailed, figures with shades of skin from alabastrine to olive. Perhaps Madonna and some other figures. Or an adult Jesus with other lesser beings. Or the last supper with the 12 diners hemmed between other nondescript human forms. Or fig-leaved Adam and Eve and the inevitable serpent and a multitude of biblical figures. Or an imagined joyful heaven with its *dishabille* occupiers. I truly can't remember the exact things I saw, a pretty impressive *staffage*, I am certain, but I can't hang together anything definite – even so an image of winged cherubs and seraphs, intermingled with sturdy humans, keeps coming to me. I had considered the picture surreal and dreamy at the time – or maybe it was only a modernist muddling and mosaicking of the ceiling of the Sistine Chapel, dense-seeming to my child eye.

Then came the Year of the Comet. I began to turn out as the bookworm of the family from early childhood and like many book-readers for book-reading sake, sometimes I tended towards scattershot encyclopaedism (if there was Wikipedia it would be Wikipedism), volubility, if not smarty-pantsiness. I remember reading about an early HIV case in an American news magazine as far back as 1981. Mentally, I encrypted the information, left it latent in my mind. Even when I had my first girlfriend a few years later, I remembered bragging to her that I knew far more about intimacies than I really knew and added, with a kind of misplaced and unintended dark humour, that I knew about every sexually transmitted disease, even a 'new' one called AIDS, and further darkening the humour was the fact that I wasn't an avatar of condom-using at the time, new as I was to fleshly pleasures.

It was in one of such newsmagazines that I had read extensively about the comet – and in *Awake*, the Jehovah's Witnesses' subsecular pamphlet. Almost every day Jehovah's Witnesses used to pad the streets of the town, doing their own curious kind of soft-conversion and sappily persuasive preaching. I remember how they were, their M.O: the gentle knock on the door, often a woman paired with a man, the man carrying a handbag, the lack of apologies, the subtle introduction of what they were there for, the bland persistence in getting across their kind of Christianity. There was something about the Witnesses which reminded me of the stoical early Christians whom Emperor Nero fed to lions. I often listened to them, weighing what they said about heaven and hell, about sin, about Jesus. Often it was a one-way affair, they just droned on while I listened, but sometimes I would interrupt and ask such a question as why their views about the divinity of Jesus were different from those of the majority of Christians. I did not get any answer memorable enough for me to repeat here. Or maybe I didn't really care deeply about the significance of such fundamental theology to properly ingest it. Evangelical churches had begun to grow in Nigeria, steadily, and the so-called spiritual ones were taking deeper root, giving people an alternative to such orthodoxies as the Anglican, Catholic and Methodist churches. But while the budding evangelical and spiritual churches were fairly accepted, the Jehovah's Witnesses were seen as a rather strange, nonconformist, fringe lot. There was the view that even if they were not exactly a cult there was something mildly weird about them, something contrary and rather proto-Christian. Although a couple of the evangelical churches were headed by highly educated men, the membership of most of the churches was culled from the lower-middle class and the working-class, yet more so for the 'spiritual' churches. There was a sort of high-churchiness about the membership of the Protestant and Catholic churches. You would not see a Yoruba high-chief or 'king' or tycoon, or the generally genteel, attending a spiritual church, and memberships of secret societies – like the freemasons – were inevitably tied with belonging to the orthodox churches. Teachers and professionals of a certain age and stature like my parents might also not consider becoming evangelical or 'spiritual,' still less gathering with the Witnesses.

This must have somewhat rubbed off on me and may have been part of the reason I did not listen to what the Witnesses were saying while tolerating them and freedom of expression. After their religious speeches the Witnesses always offered two colourful pamphlet-size magazines, *Awake* and *Watchtower*. I often chaffered with the Witnesses over why the magazines were not given away for free. They always came back with how high the cost of production was, how the magazines were worth more than the pittance they were sold for. And truly the magazines were cheap, each sold for a few pennies, cheap enough for me to be able to buy the two at once just about the age of 15. What struck me about the magazines was the pictural collage set against stories, especially in *Watchtower*, formalised treacly and florid pictures of heaven, Eden, prophets, animals mingling with humans in paradise, smiling faces, several clothed Adams and Eves holding hands, their children feeding lions and running around with tiger cubs. The contents of the magazine were no less fanciful, snippets of millenarian rapture, of prophetic guesswork served as certainties and every kind of end-time phantasmagoria. I bought *Watchtower* once but I continued purchasing *Awake*, which was considerably more secular than its sister publication. I think the romantic in me saw something in some of the happily-ever-after, exceedingly cheery, stories in the magazine, and the curious side of me also found something to enlarge the imagination in the stories of miracles, chance meetings and highly Christianised affinities. There were also some endpieces, thumbnail reports about world events, captured with cartoonish illustrations, which in spite of its slight eschatological slant, were of much interest to me. I read about the oncoming Halley's Comet in one of these titbit columns in *Awake*. There was the temporal astronomic information about the comet; then there was the oracular sting in the tail: the comet, whenever it comes, brings with it bad auguries and zodiacal negativities, trailed by ill-wind which would blow through the lives of people if not 'nations' – to use a Nostradamic term.

Just as it was in *Awake*, Comet Halley was a big story in the media, and I lapped it up greedily, though I was intrigued more by the mathematical regularity of its cycle – its orbit every 75 or 76 years – than by its supposed aura of ominousness. The fact that the birth and death of American writer Mark Twain were coincident with the secular visitations of the comet in 1835 and 1910 was of immense interest to me. *I came in with Halley's Comet in 1835. It is coming again next year, and I expect to go out with it. It will be the greatest disappointment of my life if I don't go out with Halley's Comet.* Actually Mark Twain was born two weeks after the appearance of the comet in the 19th century and died just a day after its umpteenth perihelion. Long before the 1986 comet, I had long known Twain through the *Adventures of Tom Sawyer* and *Huckleberry Finn*, but one thing that I didn't know about him was the bracketing of his life with the span of Halley's Comet's cycle. For me this was far less humorous than impressive, not forgetting that I was only 18, bookish, considerably religious, and impressionable. While I was pretty much certain that it was no more than a happy coincidence that the comet described a parabola, no, a zodiac, a full circle, over the life of Mark Twain, I still thought it was worth waiting and watching out for.

Even if she did not tell anyone, it was clear that Mojisola no longer belonged in the Church of England when she came home for a short visit. She had become 'born-again'. She prayed a lot, read the Bible most of the time, hummed gospel songs, she turned more inwards, smiled less, chatted less, but all this did not register profoundly as it was to do later. Big Sister even spoke to everyone, calmly, about the necessity of becoming born-again, how Jesus Christ might arrive anytime soon, how there was the need for more prayers, for more watchfulness, for more godliness within the family. Now this was not as unusual as it might seem, in the1970s and '80s the seed of evangelical Christianity was taking root in the campuses of Nigerian higher institutions. I remember members of a certain Christian group who were called SUs, SU being an acronym for Scripture Union. In the days when Nigeria was an oil-rich country, members of Scripture Union were a marginal and sectish lot, their countenance and composure often mirthless, their bearing aloof, their appearance dowdy, their disposition quietist and withdrawn. Although members of Scripture Union were drawn from several evangelical churches coming up in Nigeria then, they seemed to be ruled by a common creed and scriptural signification, there was a communion of a sense of devotional novelty, of emphasis on prayer, song, prudish Pentecostalism and lack of pomp. Most of the students who became members of SU had once been second or third generation Catholic or Protestant, and in so much as people even still had time to listen to what oracles of juju and *ifa* had to say, there was no objection from parents whose children became Scripture Union members in higher schools. But even before colonialists came, freedom of worship had been a natural constituent of Yoruba mores. So long as your loved one did not become a member of a secret, puppetising, and antilife cult, there was often no cause for worry.

Big Sister's declaration that she had become born-again was fine by everyone. Truly she had become more prayerful, more pious, her whole way of looking at the Christian religion had become transfixed and her life now seemed to revolve around the 'quaternity' of the cross. I don't know how easy it was for her to slough off the surplice of Anglicanism, to unlearn the capacious and waltzing pace of the Anglican liturgy, but she seemed to have taken to a certain type of hair-shirt evangelicalism so easily. She used to be a chorister in the Anglican Church. She attended an Anglican primary school, Anglican secondary school, Anglican teachers' college, the same college Mother had attended some 30 years before. She was baptised in the Anglican Church. She was confirmed in the Anglican Church. She was teaching in an Anglican school before she returned to college. Then she gave it all up. I remember the night before she returned to college, I sat with her and Mother on the balcony of our house. As was not unusual even at the time, there was a power cut, lamp and lantern light flickered from windows opened to let in air in the muggy May night, there were stars in the sky, and a crescent moon. These 'heavenly bodies' may have turned the talk we were having to the comet. Although Mother and Big Sister may have read something about the comet, I repeated everything I knew about it. The comet's rarity, its 75/76-year round trip, the fact that it was the only comet that passes earth's orbit in the quickest time – others do take a millennium or more to come full circle. I retold the story of Mark Twain, how he came and went with the comet. And, lastly, the linking of the comet with bad luck, but I quickly pointed out that such a connection was ancient superstitious twaddle, made up during by people who understood little or nothing about comets, and I told them about the pseudoscientific untruths spread even in newspapers as reputable as the New York Times about how the 1910 comet would release pestilential cyanogenic mists, killing unnumbered people, how fear, apocalyptic fear, gripped the post-*fin-de-siècle* world. I remember Mother saying a short prayer, contra Halley's Comet and whatever cussed thing it stood for. I said a necessary 'amen' to the prayer, being a Christian in a way not unusual for a youth of my age in Nigeria, but I also added that I would look out for the comet anyway, even get a telescope to see it clearer…

Two months after Comet Halley passed by the sun, news came that Mojisola had died of malaria. Several months later I wrote what I would call my first real attempt at writing free verse. I called the poem *1986*.

All of 86 is long but at 18 in 1986
he would come within my view.
Unlike the great American, I did not ride
here on his tail and there was no going
with it nor would
the environing siblings, nor would anyone,
or so did Mother's prayer go.
I waited, nevertheless, fancying a sight bright
and brilliant, even beautiful...
We shall see.
I waited, my eyes hungered to live the picture,
touch if I could the reported beauty.
He came, humbly, shy, and I beheld
the furry rabbit-scut against the ground
of dusty dim sky – a sterile pollen spray,
fleet fleece in cloudmade smaze.
Days I stood, days he stayed – I strained,
felt nothing, scarcely saw anything clearly.
There is something fuzzily uncomely about
the Comet Halley, something blasé, I imagined...
A transient thing, lasting a secondth of a second,
and he left, slyly, like a kind of night thief
and I found him easily forgettable, ectoplasm
swimming through Lethe.

But just as quietly, the passing of Big Sister –
I flew into a rage, sprang against the sky,
I must catch the tail of the Beast, he must give
her up, but the Juggernaut was long gone, not even
a trace of its cold contrail remained and ringing
in my ears was the cackle of Thingamajig:

'Fool, you can't even fly. You are flightless.
And you will not be there when I return in 76
years, long 86ed by time.
Or even if you are there
You will be an old doddery fool, blinded by time.'

I believe I was still in the grip of helpless, impotent bewilderment when I wrote the poem, and certainly under the influence of 'metaphysical' poetry, a lot of which I was reading at university. John Donne's *Death Be Not Proud* was quietly and subtly descanting itself into my head as I wrote, however *1986*, though freely written, was hardly spontaneous. Somewhere mid-scribble I had to stop myself from answering back to Comet Halley, I had to check myself from telling *him* that he had really not been successful in taking my sister away and hollering such a flaming alliterative curse of 'Heavenly body Halley rot in hell'. Maybe this is why I no longer write a lot of poems, because something as crucial as death – the loss of a loved one – and as profoundly piquant as grief can only be written about sincerely, trenchantly, with Parnassian detachment, without the tricksiness to which even the most sublime of poems is susceptible. Donne's *Death Be Not Proud* is one of the finest sonnets ever written, the personification of death is, of course, pure genius, a brilliant poetic coup, but where it all becomes a feast of stylised hyperbole is the giving of death the attribute of pride or pomposity. Death is neither proud nor unproud, death is a poker-faced automaton, nonhuman and impassible, an archetypal Godbot. Elegies, threnodies, monodies work better if death – I mean in its Grim Reaper or skeleton-suit manifestation – is ignored and the dead sung and wept for. But just as I could not easily leave the comet aside, I accepted that it is often difficult to take death for what it is: no-thing, non-entity, an abstraction.

miasma of malaria out of my space and suffused it with bracing ether. I never grew to like any other of Hemingway's books and it is no surprise that *Old Man and the Sea* is the writer's only book that I still have any clear memory of reading, and perhaps this has to do with the role it seemed to have played as connotative curative. Hemingway was no guru and *Old Man* is certainly no Veda and I don't think it gives itself the airs of hallowed pretensions or unembarrassed spiritual overtones like Herman Hesse's *Siddhartha*. I believe that fortuitously picking a contemplative novella and a compound of medicines produced a powerful psychosomatic synergy which worked well for me. Or maybe the malaria had freakishly run its course and the contents of the book were no more than a mental placebo. But this would not blind me to the danger of malaria, I realised that chances were that I would not even be strong enough to read anything if the malaria had hit hard. And then some years later my sister had to die of it.

From childhood we had begun to imbibe the ethic of using prophylactic against malaria. Quarterly, we were taken to Father's doctor friend to be dosed with chloroquine solution, or to a chemist, or a mere licensed medicine seller. Such was the fear of malaria and the damage it could wreak that Father's doctor friend even taught him how to use the syringe to give his children the anti-malarial jab if it came to a pinch, something that my other big sister, the Independence Baby, when she later became a nurse thought was a reckless and dangerous flouting of the Hippocratic Oath by the doctor. But then the fact that Father would go out of his way to line up his children and give them shots of chloroquine made an impression on us: malaria was something to be fought off at all costs. I think Big Sister was doing exactly that until she joined the evangelical church and became born-again. Even as I write I do not know the name of the church, I never bothered nor cared to know its name, nor will I ever care, but all I know is that the central article of faith of the minor denomination was prayer, intense, flagellantly passionate prayer, prayer shot through with *glossolalia* and gesture, the religious equivalent of heavy-metal headbanging. Every life's problem must be solved with prayer, everything from insomnia to malaria, and among other peculiarities, they had this Witnesses-like fundamentalism which anathematised medication. A few months after she became a member of the church, Big Sister was struck down with malaria, and when she died two weeks later from malarial complications the members of the church were blamed for not taking her to the hospital when her condition worsened. But it had all begun when Big Sister took ill and she, together with her fellow church-members, decided that prayer would heal the malaria – that was the point of no return. Malaria is infinitely lethal, it kills millions of people every year, and to leave it to the whim of prayer is tragic in the least. The concert of prayer must have been vociferous indeed because, considering the brutally incremental and degenerative nature of malaria, its access may come under what in classical medical parlance might be described as *foudroyant* – occurring suddenly and acutely like lightning strike. Even if the mosquito bites do not happen in a flash, the effect and devastation, when the *P.falciparum* parasites sink their fangs in, can be pretty swift and merciless. I do not know what happened in the last days when the malaria would have done a complex of damage: whether Big Sister had wished to be taken to a hospital; whether she had had any regrets that she had agreed to the rejection of medical treatment over against that of prayer, a prayer which was in fact a prolonged administration of extreme unction; whether she accepted with quiet grace, with Socratic stoicism, or with some Jesus-like bewilderment-unto-submission. It is impossible to know these things, just as it is difficult to blame my late sister for whatever decisions she made during the last days of her life. Vicariously, I now have the luxury of hindsight and if I had been in her position, completely consumed by religious fervour, by spirituality, perhaps I would have thought or believed a power beyond mere material things like tablets would do the job, would perform the miracle of killing off the malaria parasites. I was, myself, a Christian then, though far less devout than Big Sister. Such is the hold of religion and its matter-of-course pre-eminence that though I never saw Father strike the pose of a praying-mantis at any time while I was growing, there was a tacit assumption that he was Christian – and he might well be – but seeing the grandmothers, Mother and then Big Sister taking their prayers seriously must have had some impact on me. Between the ages of 14 and 19, I think I prayed every night or every other night, and less so on mornings.

However, the church my sister belonged to did something I consider cruel, if not perverse. Although information technology was still in the crudely telephonic stage, it wouldn't have been difficult for any member of the church to which Mojisola belonged to think of communicating with her folks when she was worsening, even if they thought praying was the right thing to do. By the time they alerted the college authorities it was too late. There was a forlorn-hope attempt to take her to a hospital. She died on the way. So within a few hours of us knowing she was ill, she was gone. She died on a Friday night, at a time, by simple straightforward coincidence that I was routinely praying before going off to sleep. I do remember that one of the strong points of my prayer at the time was the calm and self-assured invocation of God to protect my siblings and myself from any danger or ill, and on that particular night the prayer was rather lengthy, reflexive, acute and almost forethoughtful in its anxious translucent wanderings. Although I wasn't attending church regularly, there was a certain depth and solemnity about my prayers just around the time. Even after my sister died I imagined I might have had a presentiment, a dim hunch about what was going to happen. And as it inevitably transpired, I briefly thought that perhaps I had not prayed enough, that maybe if I was more passionate, more lachrymosely supplicatory, if I had mentally whipped myself up into an apotheosis of beatific preternaturalness, reached beyond *mere* Christianity, if I had enhaloed myself in the n*th* dimension of spirituality, then maybe my prayer would have worked, miraculously – although it was likely that if there was such a miracle, the church people praying for her would take all the credit for it. Anyway, this self-admonition was swept away quickly when I remembered, with some disappointment, that after all the spiritual absorption in the Garden of Gethsemane, even after the last minute appeal to God to spare his life, Jesus himself had to die, his father in heaven had 'forsaken' him. Now something that may have been simmering beneath the surface began to stir: I second-guessed myself on the virtue of prayer, I wondered what kind of prayers was answered and what kind was not.

Nevertheless for the next 15 months or so, I continued to pray while trying to deal with the loss of Big Sister. I think William James's *Varieties of Religious Experience* tries to explain my attitude to religion in those adolescence years: curiosity, exploring the frontiers of wonder and mystery, the height of magical thinking. It must have begun when Big Sister had a child and Grandma died almost at the same moment. This was the time that I found myself in what I christened the 'alchemistic phase', thanks, peripherally, to Carl Gustav

Jung. Mine was a mind bowled over with infinite possibilities. I was reading a lot of books. I had discovered the factitious mystic, Lobsang Rampa, newspapers and magazines were full of advertisements of talismans to be sent from India. My interest in the junior secondary school subject called 'Integrated Science' was sky-high. I had just read about Thomas Edison and his thousands of inventions, so it wasn't long before I turned a corner of the room I shared with Akin into what I called a laboratory, lighting bulbs with zinc and copper coins dipped in lime or salted water in makeshift beakers, trying to create filaments and tungsten out of scavenged objects, putting together a mini dynamo from coils of copper and magnet.

Then there was Christianity. There was the sense of ancestral homage. And I think I must have read about alchemists somewhere without fully grasping that they did not really succeed in turning base metal into gold and that homunculi only existed in their phlogiston-filled heads. When Grandma died I imagined she had entered another dimension, a metaphysical ghostly dimension, she had become an invisible link with the otherworld, now *Shekinah* could be channelled through her. With a view of filigreeing out my own talisman without having to send any money to India, I did something which bore on mumbo-jumbo and elaborate abracadabra. Somehow I got hold of a gold-plated bangle among many left by Grandma, cut it into a finger-ring size and marinated it in olive-oil chrism, using a china sugar-pot as receptacle. After some three days in which I engaged in wishful thinking which I otherwise thought to be a kind of theosophical meditation, I took it out, wore it on my first finger. For a week or so, before the ring went astray and never to be found again, I was awash with a feeling of self-satisfaction. Now I had been able to acquire a talisman without having to pay an extortionate fee to an unknown guru or swami in India, or his supposed representative in Nigeria. There was a sense of elation too, something that verged on beatific self-bedazzlement, I made the ring into a kind of legal high, a kind of euphoriant, because in that week I thought I was the smartest boy in the whole world. Advertised Indian talismans often promised the blessing of instant abundant wealth to their buyers, or the ability to charm (for adolescents and young men) or snare as many girls as possible, or to confer the gift of the gab which might be the reason the buyer never had a girlfriend, or yet again confer the strength packed in the horn of a rhinoceros, or for secondary school students like me, the prowess, the effortlessness, to pass examinations. But I did not wish or pray for any of these. The desire to be wise, to be smart, had somehow eclipsed what should have interested a boy of 13 whose hormonal capillaries were forgathering at the wellspring of the middle extremities, a time when Romeo-like caprine rage should have taken precedence. Of course these feelings were there, flowering, but I had thought wisdom was more important to ask for than the empowering mojo to win the *beauty* of the town. But then again the wish to be an *enfant savant* was not as original as it might appear, the influence was biblical. The story of Solomon had made a deep impression on me, but again not so much his supposed wealth and power, not his polygamy, not even his apparent satyriasis – which of course would be something my enlarging heterosexual consciousness would wish for, a thousand women in a harem – as his pansophical wisdom and statesmanlike savvy. I can no longer recall the weight of the volume of wisdom I lugged around in my head in the week that I wore the self-made talisman before it disappeared.

By the time Mojisola died a few years later, what remained in my inturned Christian eye were just several diamonded specks of religious wonder, ghostly opalescent nits of piety, and although I was still a regular, even zealous, praying being, churchgoing had become rare. Although her death was linked with religion, or too much of it, I had no problem setting the matter of belief aside in dealing with her loss. But then without realising it, my initial thoughts had erred on the side of philosophy. I had begun to tweak my consciousness into accepting that there is no gradation or order to how humans are processed through the banausic mill of death. Slowly I had begun to lift the blocking, the psychological baffle I had placed between me and this articulate reality, I had begun to accept that we lived in a world in which a child might die before his parents, before his grandparents, and that nothing, not in the least prayer, would be able to smooth the alogical warp. The acceptance of this paradigm derangement did not offer any reason or justification or even understanding, it only set my mind at the ready for the chaotic inconstancies of human existence. Largely it brought to bear on my mind the fact that life, animate existence, is ephemeral.

When one loses someone as close as a sibling, the burden of once-shared and diffuse but now wholesale concentrated memory might put itself in the way of mourning. There was the siblings' picture we took when I was still the last child shows me caught in that tableau of unruliness you'd expect of a three-year-old in front of the camera, and the twelve-year-old Mojisola holds me against her knee, tries to keep me still, she struggles to make me behave. I was too little to remember when the picture was taken, and the last copy of the picture may even have been misplaced many years ago, I have a total recall of every detail of the picture, every expression and posture.

And there is the story of how I almost handed to myself on the plate the nickname 'Big Girl's Blouse' on my first day in secondary school when I wore a top that was a cross between a shirt and a blouse, a sort of old-type shirtwaist styled with raised slightly gathered shoulders. The shirt/blouse belonged to Big Sister. All through the long school holiday I had been preparing and looking forward to secondary school, to the first day as a post-primary-school scholar, the first step to becoming a student, ceasing to be a mere pupil, because people believed that you graduated from being a pupil to a student when you entered secondary school. I remember Mother bringing in measures of the school uniform from the cloth-seller, green khaki to be made into shorts and chequered pink-and-white rayon to be sewn as shirts. That was four weeks before schools resumed, well enough for the tailor to make two pairs of school uniform for me. But the tailor, whom Mother was using for the first time because her old tailor had left town, turned out to be unreliable and in spite of the pressure Mother put on him, nothing was ready on the big Monday I would begin secondary school. This threw everyone into a spin, there was no way I was going to miss the first day in secondary school, I had insisted on that. I wanted to see how the school looked, to smell the air of the school, to walk the grounds. I wanted to cease to be a mere pupil and I was ready to clam up, sulk, sob, even blubber if I did not attend Owo High School that day, an institution with an American lexical peculiarity of 'High', which set it apart from others with the tags like 'Comprehensive' or 'Grammar' or 'Academy', Briticisms which are ultimately as irrelevant as American 'High' in schools' common curriculum. I could not have cared which school I went to so long as it was higher than a primary, or perhaps there was the implicit wish to completely rid myself of the label of 'Headmaster's Son' or

'Headmistress's Son', something that was stamped on me for most of primary school, so there was simply not going to be any question of missing the first day. A reasonable knowledge of philosophy would have told me that any day I went would have been my first day, even if it was a month after schools opened for business. A bit of cosmological physics would also have suggested to me that there is no such thing as 'first' day in the spatiotemporal corner of the universe we occupy. But then the realms of conceptual philosophy and cosmological physics were as far-flung from each other as they were from me at the time.

The tailor had again promised that the uniform would be ready for collection midmorning of the day of resumption, the special day, and I would only be late by a couple of hours for school. I refused. I wanted to be present at the gates of the school just as they opened. Mother knew I was as unfussy as any of her children, so she played along with my pointless ceremonious paltriness. I could easily have snapped out of this brattish mode if Father was called in to talk to me. Or maybe Mother realised I might truly be impatient to join my brother Akin in Owo High, he had been attending the school for a year, and we were, of course, still the best of playmates.

Big Sister had freshly graduated from a teachers' college and was home on the red-letter day I was burning to start school. She was with Mother in the room during this palaver on the eve before secondary school. She had at first suggested that I wear Akin's other set of school uniform. But I don't think they would be surprised that I refused because what would be the point of being new, of being a fresher, a plimsolled tenderfoot, in 'high' school if I donned my brother's fading one-year-old school uniform, a veritable reach-me-down? I must be mint new, spick-and-span, crisp. After several tries of possible temporary uniforms, the most plausible one turned out to be a pair of unworn wheyey chino shorts that Mother had bought off the peg that I had not got round to wearing. For some time we could not find any shirt that went with the shorts – especially a white shirt, since schools allowed students to turn out, temporarily, in white in lieu of school uniform. Then Big Sister had remembered she had a shirt, though somewhat blousy-looking, but a top nevertheless, it was what was called 'house-wear' when she was in the teachers' college, the blouse she wore over a skirt in the college dormitory and sometimes to church on Sunday. She had three but she had only worn two. She brought out the new shirt/blouse. It was pristine, but when I looked closer it appeared somewhat like a girl's blouse. I had my doubts. Wasn't it really better not to go to school at all than appear in a girl's blouse? But now I was getting tired of it all, I was wearying of the pernickety choosiness which was not something that I displayed every time. I chastened myself: now enough of this faff-around. But the desire to be present at school on the first day remained strong, so I agreed to wear the shirt, blouse really. The next morning, I blindly tucked the white blouse into my white shorts, put on my ravishingly white tennis shoes and white socks and made off to school all on my own, not even waiting for Akin. I felt wearing a potluck shirt, or blouse, which belonged to my sister, was better than having nothing to wear and not attending school on the first day.

The balloony high of being a secondary school boy was pricked during the school meal-time break. Among a group of senior students sitting on two benches under one of the many trees in the school compound, a stocky teenager beckoned to me. Tentatively, pretty much timorously, I approached them, wondering what they were up to, whether it was the norm for seniors to call juniors as if they owned them. When I got closer, I recognised the boy who called me, he was about 16, in final year, he lived in the same street as I, and he knew I had big sisters. The first question he asked almost crushed me with its brutal bloodyminded casualness. He said, not even with any irony: 'Are you a girl?'

I was dumbfounded, stricken, stupefied. Me, a girl? Growing up in a society where lines separating the genders were not meant to be crossed, I considered this a baffling question indeed.

'You are wearing a blouse, can't you see? Which sister does this belong to? The older one or the younger one? You are wearing your big sister's blouse. Or are you one of those who have a prick and a cunt? Hermaph... or what do they call the?'

I sidled away, pursued closely by the terrible-sounding teeheeing of the boys – the only girl among them had appeared curiously expressionless and coldly gracious when I stood before them, before the bar of the mocking killjoy seniors, although as I toddled away I thought I could hear her snickering. Bruised, I returned home before the school closed and did not tell Mother and Big Sister about how it might have been clear to everyone but me that I was wearing a girl's blouse. Or was it the girl who showed no emotion when I was standing before the boy who recognised the shirt for a blouse? This would have been no less awful: so every girl who saw me that day would know I was wearing a blouse. And even if I had run into a word like hermaphroditism at the time, the meaning was likely to be lost on me, but I understood the words 'cunt' and 'prick', their all-but-taboo unrepeatableness. Why did the seniors have to be so rude? Although I was rather rattled by this gaggle of foulmouthed teenagers, I made a decision before I got home that if that was the way seniors were then I would have to prepare to do battle with them, after all I taught a girl some lesson only a couple of months before on my last day in primary school. Oh, the girl – or was it a kind of retributive payback for me, karma? I beat up a girl and I was verbally being beaten up for wearing a girl's clothing. Or maybe that was a price to pay for being pig-headed about presenting myself at the school at any cost on the morning of the first day. The tailor had personally brought my school uniform in even before I returned. Quickly, I disembarrassed myself of the blouse and tried on the shirt. After I donned the uniform the next day, I completely forgot how I had turned out just some 24 hours before.

I didn't breathe a word about the matter to my sister and mother until three years later when I told Mother and Big Sister, with a certain po-faced calm, that there was a possibility that I might grow up to become a transvestite; I had used the exact word, transvestite, a word that I was pretty sure might not be familiar to both of them. I had just read the first of every book by Quentin Crisp that I was to read and had been transported into the weird world of cross-dressers, poofs, queers, mincesters, rouged and raddled old queens. I explained to Mother and Big Sister that a transvestite is someone who wears male and female clothes, who uses make-up, wears high heels, paints her lips, who walks and talks like a girl. While Big Sister found it a bit amusing, Mother was considerably horrified. Why would I do such a thing? I told her that I'd read it in books that in places like London some men sometimes wore women's clothes and that they were called drag queens – it was my desire to become the first open drag queen in Nigeria. Mother snorted words 'Impossible' and 'God Forbid', making a pooh-poohing gesture of swishing her left arm in a spherical circle over her head with a loud fillip, a vigorous demonstration of rejecting something out of hand. Then to push further the matter of my cross-dressing future, I came close to home. I reminded Mother that the male 'king' of Owo and his chiefs wore crinoline-puffed skirts during a certain annual festival, and they also had their hair plaited like women, so it was not only in London that men wore women's clothes. But then, Mother argued, I wasn't going to become an Owo chief; even so the drag was only an occasional costume for the chiefs, and they didn't wear lipsticks and heels like I said I would. Big Sister, calmer, and more in tune with my ability to be arch and cheeky, even grimly wicked, asked why I thought I might become a drag queen. I said that it all began with her giving me her blouse to wear to school on the first day of secondary school. Clearly, I could that see she could not recall this, nor could Mother. I reminded both of them of what happened. While Mother looked at me with a kind of concern and a tincture of apprehension, Big Sister just couldn't find it in her heart again to smile. I realised that they were taking me too seriously and I decided to put them at their ease: I was only joking about becoming a cross-dresser, and I understood that it was inevitable that I should wear the blouse on that first day at school, there was nothing to feel guilty about. Even now I understand the good intention, the love and altruism, which impelled both women to find something for me to wear when I insisted on attending school.

Big Sister attended the same teachers' college Mother had attended more than a quarter of a century before, St Mary's, an Anglican institution which neighboured on the high school I was just starting. Akin had enjoyed a whole year of stopping by to say hello to Big Sister and eat rice dressed with dodo and black-eyed beans, buttered crackers, cakes, buns, egg-rolls and drink Coca Cola or cold cocoa. He always came home to tell him me how Big Sister made sure his stopovers were filled Lucullan indulgences. I salivated for all of these things, and envied Akin. Unfortunately, Big Sister was in her final year when I was preparing to go to secondary school. By the time I would start, Mojisola would have graduated. I expressed how I found this ruefully painful and sad, but we realised that I had just one chance to drop by to see Big Sister while returning home from the secondary school. I would be paying a token visit and touring the new school, this was an invitation extended to every prospective pupil, when one would be walked round the school grounds and given the school's prospectus. As it happens, the day I would go for the visit was Mojisola's last day in the teacher's institution. To compensate for the fact that I would not be stopping by to eat sumptuous foods and munch on every sort of toothsome refection on my way home from school for even a term, she promised to wait for me to finish my tour of Owo High School. She would prepare a variety of food, a princely spread of delicacies, everything from coconut-flavoured rice richly topped with diced beef marinated in mulligatawny-type soup with emphasis on tomato rather than chilli, to sautéed sliced bread and noodles steeped in minestrone soup, to sardine-sandwich bread, washed down with fresh orange or mango juice, and then finished off with a dessert of cocoa mousse. Apart from the joy of having Big Sister cook such meals for me, the variety of food she promised to prepare was not something she and all of her brothers and sisters would have every day at home. But as a student away from home she had the freedom to spend her money on as much delicacies and beverage as she liked, even an exotic food like pasta. And that would have been the first time I would eat pasta, which was not a local dish by any means, and she was not just thinking of doing mere tomato-topped pasta, but richly-stuffed *agnolotti*.

This tantalisingly envisaged first taste of pied pasta would be put backwards a few years because while touring the secondary school, I met two boys and soon we discovered that we lived just a few streets from one another, although not unusually, we attended different primary schools. Within moments of meeting we started chatting. I thought I could not be surpassed for storytelling, but when I met these two boys I was humbled. One of them, the same age as me, was a scout. He mesmerised me with stories of clumps and treks through deep, sometimes boggy, forests with fellow scouts, camping, snaring and roasting rabbits and fat rodents, hunting antelopes, killing boars, singing, and sitting round fires at night. He told colourful stories about big scout jamborees he'd attended, and he started to do all this when he was only six because his father was Scout Master and he took him along during scout trips. The other boy was about 14, having spent time in Secondary Modern before he came to secondary school. The second boy held my attention as rivetingly as the first one and now in a wide-eyed slobbering way. He had a girlfriend, had had two girlfriends before that, and he had opened up to me a world of bulbous and tussocky mysteries, of haptic ecstasies, of eruptive seizures, of dark rooms and deep recesses, describing the hidden meaning in the drift of birds and the drone of bees. Travelling to school in a car and going to eat midday meals in my father's office were tame and infantile beside the exhilarating retellings of these boys' extraordinary life stories. The only narrative I had in my head was how I beat a girl up, which might not be that interesting, and somehow none of the adventures I always took from the books that I read had come up to my mind. I suddenly dried up. The second boy was telling the story of his girls when we went out of the school, passed the gates to the teachers' college, and for the hour we walked home. I remained distracted by these fecund recitals of precocious conquests for an hour or so before I realised what I had done.

When Big Sister arrived home later that day, she was clearly upset with me. Why hadn't I come? What happened? She had prepared everything she said she wanted to prepare and more. She waited for me for hours, contriving ways to keep the food warm and fresh. I could not say anything but tell Big Sister I was sorry. And the food, foods, the dainties? Some of her school-friends whom she had told she was expecting her kid brother, set about the food just before she left the college for the last time. Even years after Mojisola died, what I did was still coming to me with some guilt and regret. Now it was no longer a matter of missing the food she prepared, but how I was so carried away with listening to the boys' tales, mere pabulum, candyfloss, the boys' yarns, and passed before the gates to the teachers' college. There was no explaining away my utter dissolution in schoolboys' pigswill, my thoughtless trivialisation of sibling *agape*, and I have used this term in both its plain classic sense of selfless love between individuals and, figuratively, in its early Christian sense of a communal meal in commemoration of the Last Supper. Although she died almost a decade later, this was simply the last crucial meal I never had with my sister. What was I thinking? How did I allow my mind to wander off such a dutiful date? I knew I loved Big Sister and, of course, she meant a lot to me, but somehow I forgot to redeem the promise I made to her. Today my knowledge of the psychology of attachment and loss has gone a long way in explaining what may have gone wrong, or right – forging my independence, weaning myself into personhood, dappling the shadow of Jung's 'mother complex' with the centrifugal sun of schoolboyish carefreedom. Even then, I still feel a twinge of guilt and regret for not stopping by to see my sister when I promised her I would, her loss had become coterminous, even synonymous, with that abdication of duty. Or was that why I ended up wearing her blouse on the first day of secondary school? No, I don't mean to say Big Sister had mischievous intentions, but that perhaps the *contretemps* was meant to teach me, subtly, that navel-gazing, useful as it might be sometimes, should be balanced with familial umbilical connections.

Via Dolorosa

I often make a point of saying that my sister's death had not turned me into an agnostic, an apathetic agnostic, a nullifidian sceptic, a 'bright' – to use a word some atheists are now trying to push – and I believe this is true. If I had not lost a sister at the time I did, if I had not been bereaved at 18, by the time I was 25 I would, nonetheless, have relieved myself of the millstone of religion, or got far in the gradual reappraisal of my relationship with religion, the so-called 'revealed religion' that is Christianity. But then I cannot discount the possibility that Big Sister's death and the circumstances of her passing may have been a factor – in an unconscious way – in reaching the considered conclusion that perhaps there is nothing like *God* or gods peering down on us, a god who keeps an eye out for whether I, for instance, am in the act of coveting my neighbour's sleek car or secretly ogling his wife. Now let me declare from the first that any God or god that gets himself – oh, it's 'Himself' all right – interested in such prurient and pismirish things is not worth worshipping. (Pismire is an older word for an ant, and this has just got me wondering now: how large does an ant stand – or crawl – in the eyes of the Lord? Did God really create ants, the many subspecies of ants, and every sort of animalcule? Were these things part of the twinned passengers in Noah's ark?)

Here is an alter-ego of God – possibly me – lording it over a swarm of ants, *Lord of the Ants*:

I am still winning against the little red ants
marching into my cocoa mug,
they've been trickling in for hours
seeking the sticky sweetness of the sugared lees
of milky cocoa, many dead, drowned, sunk,
many afloat, struggling like soldiers
in a stygian moat about a grand redoubt
many still marching in, dozens, scores,
coming headfirst, blind, thoughtless,
like foolhardy treasure-seeking soldiers.
I have sat for hours, beguiled,
watching, beaming, slapping my lap like a fat
war-winning General.
like Mr Jehovah cracking up
with laughter while watching
Egyptians going belly-up
in the Red Sea

Any god who also fails to get himself interested in bigger things like the rise of Hitler and how he was able to unleash horror and catastrophe in which tens of millions of people died is also not worth worshipping. Or a god who gets himself interested in things only by the dodge of some kind of warped negative theology. And what happened to my sister would have given any theologian or even a Judeo-Christian exegete, an opportunity to further split the tricky wraith-thin hair of freewill. It would be easy for the hairsplitter to place the responsibility of not accepting any treatment but opting for prayer on her. Mojisola chose the path of prayer as a curative, she placed her hope on faith – and miracle that could be the corollary of faith, something which a Catholic thinker, for instance, might not really see as a wrong path. But it is an elementary ingredient of Christianity like freewill that has turned the religion into a systematised contradictory rigmarole because it should not take a deep-thinking person to see that freewill is not altogether free of influences of every sort. With or without God, it is now received opinion that genetic factors and environment influence most of the decisions we make – and the monstrous arbitrariness of the ways of nature, which is almost the same thing as when people talk about the mysteriousness of God. Even nature is more congruous to logic than the concept of God. Nature, to a degree, is knowable, readable, and even tameable. But God is none of these, actually one of his attributes is unknowability, the nub of apophatic (negative) theology, but how anyone can reconcile this to describing him in terms like omnipotent and omniscient is beyond me. The epistemic modality used to stake these claims on behalf of God couldn't have been farther fetched. And if God is synonymous with nature as some pantheists have suggested, then he ceases to be the sentient God of Abraham, or even the rather demure 'living' God father of Jesus – which is pretty much what Baruch Spinoza says with a certain amount of casuistry in his *Ethics*. But it was actually not the questioning of the attributes of God that finally nudged me over on the side of scepticism. The act of slinking through the wormhole spatially linking the brambly, if deceptively soft, rose-bed of religion with the hard sleepless flinty bed of unbelief had nothing to do with God. It was the concept of religion, what I thought was the imposition and spoon-feeding of religion at an age in which I, literally, didn't know my right hand from left. Although I do not disagree with archatheist Professor Richard Dawkins about a lot of things, his views on the immersion of a child in religion since the first few years of her life is something that I share wholeheartedly. I called myself a Christian for the first 20 years of my life not by my own choosing, but because my parents felt it was natural to have me baptised three months after I was born, because they allowed me to be dipped in the church stoup, allowed a pastor to place a hand on my head.

At the time I was born, issuing birth certificates was not that common, so in spite of being born in a Catholic hospital run by nuns, I had no birth certificate. But I still have the original baptismal certificate, issued by the Anglican Church a few days after I was born and it has been put to good use, having done duty for birth certificate a number of times. My baptismal name was Oluwaseye. When I asked Mother why none of her children had 'Christian' names like Michael or Peter in their baptismal certificate, she told me that Father had objected to giving his children what he considered foreign names, names that might indeed be meaningful in an obscure Christian sense, but could easily be replaced with Yoruba names that had God infused somewhere. For instance, Oluwaseye – *The Lord gives glory*, which would have translated, roughly, as *Victor*, because I am not sure you can call a male child Glory or Gloria. But I have given up Oluwaseye, not just because I now look askance at the thesis of God dishing out glory in any measure, and I am not sure, knowing what I now know – and do not know – about 'God,' that he would easily give away the boon of glory to a tot of three months whom he might even kill off before the tiny thing could enunciate 'G'. (What and who kills babies really? Maybe it's not God. The Devil. Death. Accident. Herod. Moloch. Anything but God.) Again, I do not need any middle name, the surname Oriku is one of the rarest among the Yoruba, the likelihood is that even now I might be the only Adebowale Oriku who lives in the UK, save my sons who both bear the middle name Adebowale, a name-giving quirk that owes everything to their mum. And, curiously enough, my father, despite rejecting classic Christian names for their exoticism when it came to his children, retained his given name of Jacob. It is clear why Father was called Jacob: from Jacob in the Bible. As it happens, the story of Jacob and Esau is one of the most counterintuitive in a book that is full of so many antiheroic yarns. Knowing him as I did, Father would have examined the story of Jacob and Esau closely too, and I have a feeling that smouldering somewhere in the man's soul – qua soul – was doubt, an unexpressed theological doubt; or perhaps he was a man struggling with the 'doubt of his doubt' as his favourite author, Graham Greene, put it.

Ours was not a household where children were compelled to say grace before meals or gather together at night to pray, but my earliest conscious exposure to religion was seeing Mother kneeling by her bed and praying last thing at night and first thing in the morning. Also significant was the experience I garnered while following Father from primary school to primary school. Although churches were still hugely influential in the running of 'faith' schools when I started primary school, the country's military rulers had by then decreed that government had as much stake and influence. Unlike how it was in the 1950s and early '60s when Catholic teachers had to work in Catholic schools, a teacher who was recognisably Anglican could be 'transferred' from an Anglican school to Catholic or Methodist and vice versa. I started school in St Andrews Anglican Primary in whose large compound was the stone-built church officiated by an archdeacon, a church which later became a bishopric. I have as much memory of the school as of the church, or churches – because there was also the old adobe-built barn-like church, a rather plain ark with old wood-panelled casement windows and doors, and fanlights tucked high in the wall. The church became a structural sidekick after the bigger cathedral church was finished, just about the time I started school. The old church was later used as Sunday school and years later, during school days, it would be divided into three classrooms – in spite of the bouncy acoustics, constant sound-wave interference, and the shadowiness of the interior. Even when all the windows were open, there was always a dusky character about the guts of the church, there was a grisaille depth, a sable backcloth sometimes brindled with streaks of daylight from open windows and doors. The place would compose well for the palette of a tenebrist painter, a latter-day Caravaggio.

After the new church was built, the old one took the name Children's Church. We did not attend church every Sunday, maybe two Sundays in a month. I attended few Sunday schools in the old church. I never really liked to go into the church. I had the choice of either following Mother into the new-built big church and sitting among glum unsmiling adults, or going into the old one and mixing with children and being told cautionary fables and morality tales out of the Bible. I often chose the old church not so much because of its lighthearted Sunday school service, or because it gave me the opportunity to shirk attendance and play truant in the church/school compound, but that during the time I was free to roam I could skulkingly spend the offering money Mother gave me on roast peanuts and honeyed parched corn. At both sides of an arched gateway that led only to the old children's church there were two Hausa women who sold these incredibly delicious peanuts and corn. In the few years of childhood that I went to church with Mother, hardly did I put down any money. If I looked forward at all to going to church it was because it would provide an opportunity to spend the Sunday money on these titbits, the anticipation of the savouriness, the tastiness of the snack. During the Sunday school singing session, a song often repeated goes this way:

God's money
Do not use God's money
To buy crisps,
God's money
Do not use God's money
To buy sweets,
God's money
Do not use God's money
To buy peanuts…

Even now I do not know why I scarcely scrupled at using God's money to buy peanuts, I might just as well have begun to nurse a sneaking suspicion that it was not likely that my little-boy's mite, a couple of pennies, mere birdseed, would actually reach God's colossal hand. I might as well be thinking that God would have an abyss-deep pocket anyway, and the measly stiver I had to give would mean nothing to him. And though I did not attend a lot of Sunday schools, I knew the story of the two thieves crucified with Jesus pretty well. While the thieves must have committed a crime greater than spending God's money when they were little, at least one of them believed there was something about Jesus than met the eye, an expression of faith which earned him a passport into paradise. I might as well end up in paradise too, I may have thought, if all it took was to tell Jesus in my heart that 'You are the saviour. Truly you are the son of God.' Or maybe my laxness of manner to it all could only have had to do with the fact that in an empirical sense children are atheists, not in the way of denying the possibility of God, but in not giving any sort of consequential weight to the idea of God, I mean children of about six or seven, the grey borderland between the Age of Innocence and the Age of Fear.

The bigger, newer church held a certain fascination for me. Perhaps because it was a Christian church in the most fundamental sense, the outer walls were a mosaic of rough-cut stones, flecked, crenellated grey granite. Even if it was not built on a rocky ground, the church itself was rock, or that was the impression its builders wanted to make. The builders must have had an eye on the future of the edifice when it would come into its own as a bishopric. It had all the works: the spire, the cruciformity, the breadth, the majesty. And the inside of the church: the pews, the eagle-headed lecterns, the stained glass, and the vaulted parquet-like ceiling made with thousands of pieces of lacquered wood. I spent a lot of time admiring the ceiling, wishing that I could levitate and touch it, stroke it, float under it, like a kind of god looking down on the worshippers down below. But, of course, my feet always remained on the terrazzo floor, cool and clean – I ritually took off my sandals to feel this, caress the lapidary smoothness. I also studied the grown-up congregants, how solemn every face was, as if they were not meant to smile in a cathedral, how everyone always turned out in their Sunday best and sheen, perfumed and powdered, as if God would suffer nothing if not glad rags. There was the train at the start and end of service, and the accompanying processional and recessional. I loved to watch this pageantry pass through the central aisle of the church. The choir would come in first and then a gradation of clergy, from lay-reader to mitred archdeacon, would shuffle in as the congregation stood to watch in apparent reverence. I never failed to wonder at what power and pomp, what spirituality, the man bringing up the rear possessed, the archdeacon, how close to God he was, how godly. Had he seen God like any of those men in the Bible, like Moses? And could the archdeacon ever be a woman? Could any of the clerics shuffling into the church be a woman? The only women I saw in the procession were among the choir. Big Sister, Mojisola, was a chorister in the church during her teenage years and I'd watched her shuffle into the church with others.

After the choir, then it was a well-compartmentalised string of men wearing gowns. Why do they have to wear such clothes, I would ask myself? But then I was able to give an answer to my question easily: why do we wear *buba* and *sooro* and the white man wears a suit? Something that genuinely puzzled me was how men had to take their hats and caps off before entering the church and keep their heads uncovered for the duration of a service and women doing the opposite; the opposite sex must keep their heads covered – with anything, scarves, hats, the ceremonial crackly damask strip of cloth called head-tie. Why this ritual? Who was it for? Were there any fashion policemen and women in the church who would jump on anyone who broke the rule? Even so few broke the rule, unwittingly – a man might shuffle into the church with his head comfortably ensconced in his stylishly set traditional twill cap. A man who committed such a 'small sin' would, of course, not be strung up but from the moment he entered the church with his cap, there would be people whispering, whistling, signalling, gesturing for him to take the cap off, with admonitory faces and slightly raised eyebrows. The cap-wearer would quickly remove the cap mumbling apologies to himself, somewhat embarrassed about being so forgetful.

I used to wonder why wearing headgear or not was so important in the church. Was it because the church was a sacred place, a place of worship? Was that what God wanted, that men should leave their heads uncovered and woman should not? (Women and the problem of coverture, the problem of purdah.) Why would God be bothered about such an apparently pointless piffling thing as women covering their heads and men not covering? Or maybe it was not as pointless and piffling as it might appear. Who knew what God wanted, if he could be so concerned about the pittance I would give to him every Sunday, whether I gave him the collection money or spent it to buy peanuts? And if a man refused to take off his hat or if a woman refused to cover her head, what would God do? Would he send such a woman or man to hell? If God did not do that, as he might see those things as merely 'venial sins', what then would he do with them? What else could God do with sinners besides sending them to hell? He might turn them into pillars of salt, mightn't he? Maybe God's representatives and better-behaved children in the church – grown-ups, that is – would chuck such a person out of the church before he would whip God's anger up enough to be booked for hell. (One can see why the Catholic Church had to come up with neither/nor compromises like Limbo and Purgatory. But I'll stick with the Anglican Church that I attended as a boy.) What if a man who failed to remove his cap or hat was missed by the congregation, would God himself make a mental note and put that aside for the Day of Judgement? With the million other minor sins, infractions, big sins, bloodstained crimes and unrepeatable enormities that were being committed every moment in God's earth, would God be bothered about a man who did not take off his cap in the church? Is there anything like ancillary judgment in wherever that divine court is? Since I didn't know at the time that there was anything like man-made laws and rules, I kept the questions hanging.

Then I came to the question every child – and of course adult, godly or godless – must have asked directly or indirectly: how is God able to see everything? The problem of ubiquity and ubiety, being at once everywhere and somewhere. And other questions. Where is heaven and where is hell? Does everlasting fire really burn in a place called hell? If it burns, then how full is the place, its denizens being deathless, and what degree of burns will they sustain? Zillionth degree? How is it possible for anyone to burn forever? If it were possible, what sort of God would sit back and watch anyone he had created in his image burn and burn everlastingly? And does God really go round to hell to see how the burning of flesh, the writhing in agony, the gritting of teeth, the twisting and turning, the screams that are going on?

Actually, I went through the labyrinthine side street of hell and its flames to gain an entry into the strictured Hamlet of Fear. Some travelling evangelists had come to town one evening. One of their several venues of formalised revivals was the open ground of a non-denominational primary school close to our house. They came in big white vans rigged with loudhailers and megaphones, vociferously preaching the necessity of becoming born-again, returning over and over again to the subject of hell, how hot it is, how easy it is to be sent there after death, how someone can stay in hell for eternity, a stay of unrelieved burning and roasting, a place of gnashing and gritting of teeth and great suffering. They promised to show a film of how it looked in hell in several venues they would visit that day, how sinners would be thrown in the inferno and be left there for eternity to sizzle in their own fat and then frazzle over and over again. Whether or not they set out to make the promise of showing a film as a ploy to attract children, the primary school ground was full of children that evening. I was there with my brother Akin. While a couple of the evangelists preached, some men set up a large white-cloth screen. After some 30 minutes of another harangue against nameless sinners and their certain final one-way trip to hell, the white screen flickered and blinked, signalling the start of a short 20-minute film of Lazarus and Dives. Over the toned-down volume of the words spoken by the actors, one of the evangelists commentated and editorialised upon the film on the loudspeaker. The throaty timbre of the commentating evangelist began gently, as gently as a voice can be on a monster loudspeaker. It began to tell a starkly Manichean story, a black-and-white tale, with a good-versus-bad moral. Lazarus was poor, hungry and malnourished but righteous; Dives was rich and fat but sinful. Lazarus had nowhere to lay his head; Dives lived in a palace. Lazarus was dressed in rags; Dives was decked out in finery. Lazarus starved and did not have anything to eat; Dives feasted on ambrosia. Lazarus begged Dives to give him some food; Dives spat on him. Lazarus hungered at the gates of Dives' sumptuous house; Dives guzzled his earthly wine and gorged on his rich food. In Dives' house there were the obligatory biblical bad women, decadent, drunken, painted-up women. When Lazarus died years later, he ended up in heaven, in the bosom of Abraham, a heaven depicted as full of trees with ripe fruits, big cats playing with children, streams, warbling birds and a man and a woman looping colourful snakes around their necks (an obvious rehabilitation of the serpent in Genesis) like picturesque primordial lavalieres. The highpoint of the film was the death of Dives and his arrival in hell, wherein he was thrown straight into the flames, where he writhed in agony, bug-eyed, begging to be spared, begging to be given the chance again to live a more righteous life, hankering for a drop of water from Lazarus's finger to slake his thirst.

I returned home that night browbeaten, terrified, spooked. The imprint of hell was hotly branded on my mind, even on the distended pupil of my eyes. I all but came over feverish with the imagined molten heat of Gehenna. Formless nightmares flitted through my bumpy sleep for a number of nights after seeing the film. If this was the effect the evangelists wanted the film to have on children, then it had worked. For some time I imagined it was better to be Lazarus than be Dives, to be poor than rich, to be homeless than sheltered, to be ragged than handsomely clothed, to be leprous and scrofulous than healthy. Whenever I passed through a smithy close to our house and I glimpsed the blacksmith and his assistant pouring lava-like smelt iron, I would shudder and my vitals would momentarily warp: this is how it will be in hell, in a more vast oceanic way, a broiling, riffling sea-soup of fire. Would God punish me for spending the money I was supposed to give him on things like peanuts? Would he know? Of course, he would. God was not human, like my sister, Mojisola, who caught me one day spending the pennies I was supposed to give to God. She quietly chided me and told me to always put my money in the collection bag because God could see everything. Mojisola never told Mother what she saw me doing, and I believe she went away with that little secret. And what would God do about a little boy who appropriated the money he should give to him?

My belief-based fears were also given wings a few months later when the sort of man people from Senegal or Mali would call a marabout came to town. The Muslim holy man and magus arrived unannounced one late afternoon from the big city where he lived.

'Scourge of Kafirs' – or 'Whip of God' – was popular for not just being a brilliant Islamic scholar but also a performer of wonderful deeds. Stories were told about how he healed the sick, stopped rain from falling, conjured up stormy clouds and walked under pouring rain untouched by water. There was a tale about how he dared a gang of robbers to come to his house. The back-story is that a gang of thieves who relied on their foolproof mojo and juju-sourced daredevilry, as much as their armoury of guns and machetes, had been terrorising many neighbourhoods in the city, they were robbing, ransacking, sometimes raping and killing. The superthieves believed they were superhuman and that, thanks to juju, no knife, no bullets, no dagger, nothing would be able to penetrate their skins, still less their flesh. They battled with the police and won, outgunning them. They routed the posse of armed vigilantes who confronted them. They incantatorily fought off shamans and warlocks who tried to frustrate their intentions. And this was when Whip of God weighed in. He went to the local radio and asked the robbers, through the airwaves, why they had not come round to his house, he then said that he never locked his doors and that if the thieves came they would find the door unlocked.

The robbers were enraged, challenged, but with a view to taking Whip of God unawares they waited a full month before they paid him a visit at about two o'clock one morning. No one knew when the heavily armed band of robbers, weighted with juju amulets, bearing guns and machetes, entered the compound of Whip of God's house, but early the next morning they were found, all of 15 thieves and murderers, standing flatfooted and in a straggly way, in the large living room. They were identically mute, walleyed, motionless, spellbound, it was as if they were in the final stage of transmuting into zombies. The supposed leader of the thieves, made slightly aware by Whip of God, confirmed that they truly found all the entrances to his house unlocked, and they had gone in, intending to commit every sort of atrocity, and they all made their way towards the living room as if it was a honeytrap, they went in one after the other, all 15 of them, and after an infectious wave of fits – comparable to *petit mal* – swept through them, they all froze. The police came and took them away.

For all I know, the story of the ensnared thieves might as well be a piece of urban myth because what I had written is only one of the many threads picked out of the colourful, well-wrought tapestry of Whip of God's exploits. And even if it happened that way, he could just as well have used the trick of hypnotism to get the thieves – a feat no more than Derren Brown, the British atheist magician, illusionist and mindfuck artist, would achieve. Whip of God's long suit was jihad, war against those who worshipped other gods but Allah, although, curiously enough, his fight did not extend to Christians – possibly this was a bow in the direction of Yoruba people's age-long cultural attitude of pantheism, or henotheism. Which is where the paradox comes in: it was some of the Yoruba traditional beliefs, which preached pantheism long before Islam and Christianity came, that Whip of God fought hard to destroy.

Most of all, he fought the *Egungun*, the hierarchy of masqueraderie in the old city. In the beleaguered Yoruba tradition, the masquerader is a potent occult force, he is seen as the earthly vicar of dead ancestors and men of valour, the incarnate spirit of bygone warriors. Before the introduction of the Semitic religions of Christianity and Islam into the Yoruba society, people looked forward to the *masque* season when masqueraders would come out in the streets followed by large entourages with a lot of singing, dancing, chanting, the masquerader himself would bless and pray for people in a gutturalised voice that was meant to depict how the population of the undead residing in the Realm of Hades spoke. A town might have 20 masquerading families and between them they would create a calendar of the days each family would perform and parade the streets. Sometimes two powerful masquerading families might be booked to do the street performance on the same day, and instances of incantatory clashes were common when a masquerader would try to outmesmerise the other. In spite of the primacy of Christianity and Islam, when I was growing up in Owo, masqueraders still performed in the streets, although for children they were the ultimate bogeys, not least the younger members of the masque families who always trotted around with long willowy whips, randomly lashing out at anyone they came across. The big masqueraders were fearsome to behold, they wore the sort of masks which were believed to have given Picasso his cubist ideas, and full, sometimes pleated, many-coloured, bouffant robes, hung with curios of occultism, thatched with palm fronds. The earliest impactful turning of the screw of fear in me was inspired by the image of one of the big masqueraders that I once saw. Masqueraders, as well as things like flying pigs and every kind of chimera, flickered in and out of my nightmares for days.

Whip of God considered masqueraders heathens, evil heathens who had outlived their usefulness, who were no more than guises for worshipping other gods but Allah. He set out to fight and pulverise them to extinction. Throughout the Yorubaland, stories of spiritual confrontations and showdown between Whip of God and the masqueraders were told, how he went out with only a few assistants and recited the Koran, the hadith and whatnot while the masquerader at the head of a large following would incant and invoke words from the ancient corpus of masque mysteries. Whip of God had a running fight with all the senior masqueraders in town, a fight which culminated with a final thundery showdown with the big-gun masquerader, the king masquerader. The only physical part of the fights was the pay-off when a masquerader was unmasked – thus humanised, humiliated

Again the whole story of the fight might as well be another urban myth. But the word making the rounds was that Whip of God was travelling from town to town shining the light of Allah and belief into dark nooks and crannies, exposing the evil deeds of secret cults and picking out witches and warlocks from a crowd of thousands. When Whip of God came to town, his second-sight was lased through a house not far from where we lived. The owner-occupier of the house was a witch and the house was a coven, so said Whip of God, the landlord held evil meetings in the house. All this had come to us by word of mouth because the bearded defender of his Islamic faith always wanted to surprise the witches and wizards he intended to expose.

I left home with my brothers, Femi and Akin, and some other children in the neighbourhood to watch Whip of God in action. We found him standing on a makeshift dais in the forecourt of the male witch's house. The witch had bolted, fearing the wrath of God, to be delivered through his human Whip (this shorthand should be fine). The witch's two wives and nine children had also disappeared. As Whip stood on the dais, some objects were passed to him. One after the other, Whip showed the crowd stuff he claimed had been brought out of the house. A bongo-like drum whose head was supposedly made with human skin. A chalice – calabash-seeming but actually a halved human skull (something a certain Lord Byron used in England a couple of centuries ago). A shrunken human head. An amulet made with beaded human bone. All of these things, taken from the warlock's evil chest, were used during witch-fests and sabbats. Whip locked up the house and, with comminatory pronouncements, banished the family from returning to it.

On the way home I began to regret that I went to see Whip. The skull chalice, which might as well be a calabash, and the shrunken human head, which might be the head of a doll for it was quite small, transmuted into objects of terror. For several nights the Land of Sleep became long, tortuous and difficult to reach. I was battened down to the bed with fear, seized by the clammy, slimy if firm paws of black-cloaked bats of terror. Both the skull chalice and shrunken head floated atop my bed, almost within reach, and it was even worse when I closed my eyes, the apparitions heaved horrifyingly larger. One of the nights, when I was able to sleep, I dreamt of the shrivelled head gulping blood from the skull goblet and woke up trembling and sodden with perspiration after releasing a tiny squirt of piss.

When I was seven a pointless freak 'transfer' took the whole family from Owo to the state capital, Akure. Apart from what it did to Father's part-time entrepreneurship – a fair-sized chicken farm, a printing press, a two-truck haulage business – one of the disruptions the transfer caused was that Mother was taken away from the haven that was St Andrew's Church. She became a teacher in Ebenezer African Church School and Father became the head of St Michael's School, a primary adjunct of St Thomas Aquinas Secondary School, both of which shared the same compound as well as St Aquinas Cathedral. African Church was a breakaway heterodoxy, established by a group of African men who believed the

Church of England was too English. Like most of the primary schools adjoined to churches, Ebenezer AC was almost solely financed by the government, although the Board of Governors would mainly be members of the church. For staunch Anglicans like Mother, attending African Church was not something to consider. During the one year we spent in Akure, she never attended any Anglican church in the city, every once in a while she still contrived to travel some 25 miles to her parish to attend service. Of course, Father would not have missed churchgoing, and the fact that he had gone to become headmaster of a Catholic school would have further alienated him from dominical duties.

I followed Father to St Michael's and I still remember how every child made the sign of the cross in the morning assembly – and the prayer to Mary, a strange prayer for a seven-year-old boy who had been steeped in Anglican tradition from birth. But far more impressive for me was the sign of the cross, years after I left the school I still did the sign instinctively, automatically. St Michael is a feeder school for St Aquinas and sometimes I wondered if I would have gone on to become a Thomist of sorts, ending up in a Catholic secondary school. Well, who knows? That might have made me into a Catholic, becoming a Thomist in the fuller sense of that word. But from my reading of some of the works of Thomas Aquinas, I have no doubt that except for a major upending of my thought process, a cataclysmic moral shift, it was likely that I would become an anti-Thomist, even more likely a non-Catholic, although if I were to choose a Patron Saint in Christianity I would choose Thomas Didymus, the disciple who doubted the resurrection of Jesus and who might have become the hero of agnostics and atheists if he had doubted it to the very end.

When my parents returned to Owo, Mother was posted to St Moses Cherubim and Seraphim Primary School. St Moses was another African-initiated church, a large bethel sharing the same space as the school, but now she was able to continue attending the Anglican Church at the other side of town. Father was posted to New Church Primary School, and again I followed him to the school. This was where I spent the last three years of primary school. The school was built on a rise of land through whose lowest point a stream that had a few varieties of fauna flowed – some more adventurous pupils had been known to catch frogs, minnows and a species of pygmy cichlids, in the stream. Directly opposite New Church Primary, at the other side of a tarred road, there was Methodist Primary School and Church. I remember how I always wished to cross the road to get a closer look at the Methodist compound, but somehow I never got round to doing that.

The grounds of New Church were farther flung than Methodist's. On the other side of the stream there was a hill, higher than the one on which the school was built. The New Church building was erected on the brow of the hill, a cathedral-size church-house, unmissable even from a mile away. The first time I went near the church I had followed Father one evening during his first week as headmaster to visit the pastor of the church. The pastor was an elderly balding man wearing a black suit and a dog collar. We went into the priest's office, on the top storey of the house. There was a power-cut and the house was lit with several kerosene lanterns. In the office, three white candles burnt from stands, two on the table and one on a wooden cabinet. The office was lined with books, tomes, and it smelled of aged cellared pulp and the musk of old furniture, and I was especially struck by the silence. Are there no children in this place? I asked myself. I was answered by a silence only punctuated by the familiar voice of my father and the soft urbane voice of the pastor. When the clergyman went out to look for something I had to keep my eyes on my father for reassurance, so quiet and eerie the place had become, and in spite of the three candles burning in the office there were still small recesses of shadows. It wasn't exactly a scary or spooky place but I was slightly relieved to be out in the cool open air of the early evening again. And I can still recall overhearing the pettish comments of a teacher who came into my father's office when I was eating my midday school meal in the office a few days after we visited the New Church pastor's house. The teacher was somewhat agitated that the pastor of the New Church belonged to a cult called 'the Rosicrucians.' I remember Father dismissing the suggestion that the Rosicrucians were cultists, he told the teacher that he used to subscribe to the Rosicrucian magazine when he was a student almost 30 years before. (I didn't grow up to find any copy of the magazine in the house. What he said in the exchange between him and the teacher was all I ever heard my father say about any interest in anything tinged with religion, belief or mysticism.)

More than all, I recall the ecclesiology of the New Church building. It was not built impressively like the Church of England a couple of miles away, it possessed no masonic sublimity like the Anglican cathedral. The New Church was actually a steepled, fairly large, unplastered, rough-hewn, cement-grey chapel with unfinished stained glass and sparse appointments, completely lacking the relative splendour of the Anglican church. But the three wooden doors that led to the church made an impression on me. The wood was solid *iroko,* unvarnished, nut-brown, grainy, relieved with images of angels, saints, Christ, apostles, but there was a figure, a central patristic image, which featured on the three wooden doors. Emanuel Swedenborg. Who was Swedenborg? Why was his head carved on the door, salient, pre-eminent, sizable, even larger than life? Whenever I remembered my time at New Church Primary, I always recalled the heads of Swedenborg embossed on New Church portals, but as a little boy looking at his picture, I had a vague idea of who he might be, and then I had read his biography sometime in the late 1980s. Swedenborg, a scientist turned religious visionary, a mystical Unitarian, he was so otherworldly in his thoughts and practice of religion that some religious scholars still believe that he suffered from theomania – or what has been described as 'messianic psychosis.' I would leave revisionist psychologists to make whatever they want to make of Swedenborg's self-confessed ability to commune with spirits, angels and demons, make visits to and sojourn in heaven and hell any time he liked.

Being of African origin, I could not but be captivated with Swedenborg's foreordination of Africa as the future stamping ground of Christianity. Reading this at the time had set off a riotous simmer of blood in my fast haemorrhaging Christian soul. How good it would be if Africa became the New Jerusalem, the New Earth, the Mecca of Christianity! But this burst of elation was short-lived because one of the stronger reasons I was making the decision that religion, no less so Christianity, was not for me was how it was rip-roaringly becoming the 'new black' among people around me, how people were herding, as if driven by some kind of mass hypnosis, to immerse themselves in the splashing waters of Pentecostalism. I too, in a way not so dissimilar from Swedenborg, foresaw a sea of religiosity that would engulf Africa, in which Africans would asphyxiate and drown themselves. Swedenborg had made his more felicitous prophecy long before the powerful image of the kneeling African captioned 'Am I not a Man and a Brother?' was produced, at a time when the slave trade was at its meridian, when the degradation and dehumanisation and the Calvinistic preterition of the African were beginning to take root. I don't know how Swedenborg came to the conclusion that Africa would be the hotspot of Christianity in the future. Was it an expression of latent liberalism, or had Swedenborg truly foreseen anything? No one can tell, but between the time I read the Swedish Christian mystic's biography and now, Africa has got nearer to fulfilling the prophecy. This has been exemplified by Nigeria, exponentially and representatively. The continent has now become a widely-vistaed swath – I'd say swathe – of Bible Belt. And some parts of the continent also wear Islam as braces. Which is all very well.

A couple of years ago, an essay I wrote about the adverse effect of the efflorescence of religion in Africa in which I referred to Swedenborg's prophesy had given me the opportunity to read another work about the man. A senior figure in the Swedenborg Movement in America had read the piece, overlooked my contrary conclusions regarding the Swede's fatalistic predictions, and had sent me her book, a book that offered rather eccentric but delectable and epigrammatic insights into Swedenborg's life. In passing, the American Swedenborgian touches on the uber-Christian future that the founder of her church intuited for Africa, although while reading the book, I felt that if I had remained in the Christian religion, I might have toyed with becoming a Swedenborgian, and not so much because of his theology as for his personality, his idiosyncrasies, the quirky nature of his interests. But then when I remembered the epiphanies he claimed he had about angels, demons, heaven and hell, I wondered whether I would have stretched my reborn Christianity that far.

Many years ago, in my mid teens, it did cross my mind that if I were a Catholic I could have become a priest, inspired in this fancy by the fact that a lot of Catholic priests also belonged to the intelligentsia. There was a certain Catholic 'Father' writing prolifically and intelligently in Nigerian newspapers. There was T S Eliot, the secular High Priest of High Church (Anglo-Catholicism), and Graham Greene, and G K Chesterton, and C S Lewis – these were authors whom I read and whose Catholicism had made me think that it was possible to combine writing beautiful imaginative literature with belief in revealed religion. But then even in those days, all I had to do was to place CS Lewis's *Mere Christianity* beside Bertrand Russell's *Why I am not a Christian* to soldier on with weaning myself off the trickly consolations of religion. I was lucky to read *The Chronicles of Narnia* at the right time – in my mid-teens – but if Philip Pullman's *His Dark Materials* had been available then I have no doubt that it would have appealed as much to me as *Narnia* and would have touched as deep a chord. I later learnt that Graham Greene was no more a Christian than Bertrand Russell and that his Catholicism was only a cavalier intellectual dalliance with faith.

Mother skipped church a few Sundays in a year, maybe because she did not drive. Even then she did not take her children with her every time she went to church, often there were after-service Mother's Union briefings, YWCA meetings and so on. On a number of Sundays, Mother would send Akin and I away to New Church, which was only a few minutes stroll from where we lived, to attend service. I do not remember how the church service went, but I knew even then that it was different from St Andrew's. For instance, the pastor, who was not Yoruba, officiated in English, and there was a man interpreting for him. The New Church had fewer congregants, easily countable, and the pews, functional and bald and few, hardly ever filled, you could sit in the middle of a vacant pew if you liked to feel regal and savour your space. During one of my few attendances, a hen skittered into the church, pursued by a cock, causing some racket with their cackles and the flapping of their wings, and it had been particularly difficult ejecting the fowls. I remember this clearly because I spent much of the time in the church concentrating on everything but what was going on at the lectern and pulpit. I was distracted by the modest characterless ceiling of the church, by the unostentatious walls, the plain floor, the electric-green altar cloth, the distant sound and movement of traffic outside. But when I sneaked out of the church to wander around a bit, there were no snack-sellers around from whom I could buy sinful snacks like peanuts and honey-fondued corn.

If I had grown up in a society less saturated with religion I think I would have completely lost all interest in religious faith and belief at an earlier age, probably sometime after I realised that it was better to spend the Sunday money I took to St Andrew's on peanuts and sweetened corn than dropping it in that puce velvet bag that looked like a pendulously overweight scrotal sac. But in ways more subtle than what we have now, the consubstantiation of religion and spirituality was everywhere. Almost every morning – at about 4.00 am – one was woken up by dawn preachers who rang bells between monitions about heaven, hell, the Second Coming and the Day of Judgment. These 'prophetic' men would have run into platters of richly-prepared food placed at the epicentre of crossroads and junctions, fetish offerings to invisible nocturnal entities and spirits, although some time during the day the food was often picked up and consumed by tramps or other roaming unfortunates.

Even the secondary school I attended was, in principle, Anglican, prayers were said and hymns were sung every morning in the assembly. While I naturally joined in the rote prayers, I was not quite keen on singing any hymns simply because my preteen mind would not just bother to be interested. I lost my *Songs of Praise* hymn book a couple of weeks after I arrived at school, and I never had any hymnal in my possession for more than a few days in five years. Since it was a small book, it was not unusual to find a copy and keep it if you wished to. I found several but I only held on to them for no more than a day. Every student's favourite hymn was song 100, Isaac William's *Be Thou My Guardian and My Guide.* The whole assembly often exploded into a choral and cacophonous extravaganza whenever the officiating teacher called out 100. I only mimicked singing the praise songs, even when I had the book open in my hand, I just couldn't be bothered following the movement, and words like *Thou* and *Thine* had begun to amuse me a bit. In my first year the Gideon men had come and distributed small New Testament Bibles, burgundy-backed antiseptic-looking little books. There was no preaching, no proselytising, nothing, the men just handed the Bibles out quietly as if they knew they were giving away books that would work their wonders even if they said nothing. I had the Gideon Bible for years, and I remember the fiction-reader's pleasure I had when reading and rereading the gospels, the storytelling, of Jesus' life from birth to death.

It was during my early secondary school years that it dawned on me that atheism was humanly possible. I'd heard of Dr Tai Solarin, a man from the south-west where I was from. He was what they used to call a 'radical'. Dr Solarin was a teacher, the proprietor of a school, but he was – again to borrow another koine-word of the time – a 'social critic', he made himself the voice of the voiceless, he spoke against corruption and other 'sins' that those in government committed. He was also famous for being an atheist, a secular humanist – a rare bird in Nigeria. Although most of the articles he wrote in newspapers were pieces bemoaning one bureaucratic lapse or the other, he also wrote about his unbelief. I didn't begin to read Solarin's articles until I was in my mid-teens, in latter secondary school classes, but I knew about his plucky promethean struggles early on, the sort of direct action that saw him camping in the grounds of government offices, and not leaving until someone listened to him, or until he saw results.

By the way, I knew about and puzzled over the atheism of a woman called Miss Goddard's before I grew enough to read about Dr Solarin's unbelief with mature comprehension. Miss Goddard was perhaps one of three Europeans living in Owo at the time I started secondary school. She was English – or British, because she might as well be Scottish or Welsh – and she taught English and English literature in St Catherine's Secondary School, a girls-only institution that Big Sister, Mojisola, attended. Miss Goddard lived in a bungalow that was sentinelled by a copse of fruit trees. The house was close to Owo High School and quite some distance from where the woman taught. I used to visit Miss Goddard's house with her stepson who was living with her. Ayo was my classmate and a good friend, we struck up a close friendship during my first week at school. Something I noticed early was that he was interested in art, specifically in carving and sculpture, he even brought some artefacts to school. Ayo's father was an artist who had achieved fame and recognition home and abroad long before the country became independent. The Artist was in his late sixties when I knew the son, he was a tall gangly elderly man who often wore dark glasses and enormous ivory and silver rings on his fingers. I visited his house with Ayo many times. It was a grand house, a four-storey affair, built with unpainted concrete, looking somewhat ill-featured from outside. But I never ceased to marvel at what I saw inside the house, every wooden structure and piece of furniture was a work of art, from the main door and beyond, the panels, the pillars, chairs, table legs, bedposts, ceilings. The Artist's sitting room remains in my memory, I was at once awed and enchanted by the fabric of the commodious living space, the place was a paradise of woodwork, the polished parquet floor, the wall panels, the ceiling, and the chairs which were beautifully and austerely cushioned with earth-coloured calico. There was a sturdy pair of floor-to-ceiling wooden pillars, panoplied with images of a menagerie of animals, equatorial fauna, particularly the heads, the snarling maws of lions, the sinister rictus of cobras complete with their beamy hoods. Over the lintel of the door that led to the Artist's main bedchamber a couple of ivory tusks and an abridged proboscis jutted from a wood relief of an elephant head. There was also verisimilitude in the shape animal hides hung on the wall and laid on the floor, and lifelike stuffed animals, a couple antelopes, a hyena, a wildcat – a large head of a buffalo dominated the vast baronial sitting room from high on the wall.

If I had not just passed the Age of Fear, I would have anticipated the grotesque and zooscopic dreams that would come of all this. The Artist hated television, his son told me, but there was an early-type black shellac telephone placed on a low-slung carven stool which mimicked the Ashanti stool. A radiogram was niched inside a rustic *obeche* dugout. Ayo had told me that one of the wooden wall panels was populated with copies of artefacts 'stolen' by the British from Benin City, a kin city, culturally, with Owo. I didn't know a lot about the things taken by British invaders at the time, but I knew – or was told – that the mascot for the Black Festival of Arts and Culture, which took place in Lagos in 1977, months before I visited the Artist's house, was borrowed from the British Museum, and not even the ivory mask itself, but its image. The Artist's son told me how angry his father was that the British Museum refused Nigeria's request for the mask, which was now Britain's by virtue (some would say 'crime') of *uti possidetis*, to be taken to Lagos. But the dozen or so black-and-white pictures hung on the wall of the sitting room showed the impressive-looking Artist visiting England, among other foreign countries. He had pictures taken of himself with a number of eminent Britons (or that was the way I saw it then), and there was a snap of him in what I would call, for want of an accurate description, the 'Empire Room' of the British Museum.

I can't remember the expression on the face of the Artist, but maybe his sensitivity, the affect, even pathos, that the Benin art in the British museum seemed to call out in him was simmering during that visit. But again it might be during this visit that he met Miss Goddard and when the woman fell for him. When the Artist got together with Miss Goddard, he had four wives living in the same house as he in Nigeria. He was polygamous, and this was not so much a function of Fela-Kuti-like bohemianism as it was of pedigree and class, of received patriarchalism. He explained to the young woman, a divorcee and a votary of exotic art, that he had several wives, but the Englishwoman did not think that should be a bar to love. The Artist was what he was, a brilliant artist, even if he had four wives, she considered it a challenge to be one of the women in the harem of such a man. Miss Goddard, a teacher, decided that she would not only be the fifth wife she would also relocate to Nigeria to be with the Artist.

It was natural that the white woman, who never took the Artist's name, became the favourite wife – 'trophy wife' would be more like it. This was in colonial Nigeria when even a single man returning home with a European wife was rare, to say nothing of a man who had four wives. Even more than 20 years later when one of the artists of Osogbo took a German second wife, it made headlines. Miss Goddard was the first in the line of women who left everything they were doing in Europe, left their families and friends, to become wives of African artists, often second or third, or in the case of Miss Goddard, fifth wife. When I first saw Miss Goddard she was about 60, she was still the Artist's wife, now middle wife, because the man took another four women as wives after Miss Goddard came to live with him in Nigeria. But throughout their three-decade relationship, the Englishwoman did not live in the same house as the other wives or with the Artist and apparently this didn't affect their relationship, they pretty much lived in each other's pocket in the earlier part of the relationship. Things had mellowed by the time I knew the white woman. While the Artist's house was close to downtown Owo, the English wife lived in the suburbs, and being childless, she always had one or two of the Artist's children by other wives living with her. She chose which child she would like to stay with her and had had her favourites. Over the years, no fewer than ten of the Artist's many children lived with Miss Goddard. Ayo, my friend, became her ward when he entered secondary school. He told me the day we became friends at school that he was living with his father's English wife and that if I didn't mind he would take me to the house the next day, during school break, so that I could go and have my first ever bite of toasted bread and conserve. Or had I ever had such a delicacy?

The white woman only taught part-time in the girls' school, mornings, so whenever she was not in the house we would have a free run of the place. There were five rooms in the house, Ayo's, Miss Goddard's, Guest's, and two rooms whose walls were lined with shelves of books. I had never seen as many books as I saw in Miss Goddard's house, hundreds and hundreds of books, if not thousands. It was there that my love of books and reading notched up several gears. Although my reading taste was still embryonic and my intellectual range modest, I thrilled with elation when I beheld the books – *this is treasure,* I said to myself. What is in all those books, what stories? I asked Ayo if I could borrow a book or two from the woman's huge collection. He wasn't certain the woman would know that any book was missing from the thousands she had. He told me to take one home, read it as quickly as possible, and be sure to return it before the woman noticed it was missing. I picked *Book of Insults* and spent months poring over wicked rapier-thrusts and witty repartees robustly let loose by men like Winston Churchill and Thomas Carlyle. As the months passed, I crammed my head with acid insults and cutting quips and after a while the book disintegrated so much so that even if I intended to return it to the Englishwoman I would not be able to do so.

One day Ayo told me that Miss Goddard not only hated going to church, but also did not believe in God. He couldn't tell me more about her atheism except to show amazement at the fact that someone, anyone, did not believe in God. Innocently enough, I told Ayo he should not forget that the woman was English and might have different opinions about God. Ayo gave me an answer which I considered sensible even at the time. His mum was Catholic and he attended Catholic Church on some Sundays, the father who officiated in the church was English, like Miss Goddard (in all likelihood, the Father was Irish). I had wished I could buttonhole Miss Goddard and ask her why she was not a Christian. But since we often went to the house when she was not in, I didn't see a lot of her and even one day when I visited the house with Ayo and the Englishwoman was home, she was as elusive as a ghost in a ghosthunters' serial. I only saw her once or twice, and briefly, slippered, greying and bespectacled. And I imagine there was no way I could have asked her why she didn't believe in God even if she had deigned to pause and ask what my name was. She only shuffled by with adult disinterest. Perhaps curious to get to the root of her atheism, I went back to look at her bookshelves, and I must have seen many books which might have influenced her thinking, but I remember that when I glimpsed *Why I am not a Christian* I did a doubletake to be sure that Miss Goddard was not the author. The book was written by someone called Bertrand Russell. I took it out and when I got home I discovered that, although I understood every word of the couple of pages that I read, this was a book for grown-ups. I was only 11 and I knew that there was something pellucid and pleasant about the way the author wrote, but I still could not follow his argument. I read *Why I am not a Christian* a few years later after Dr Tai Solarin named it among the books which influenced him.

When I was reading it, I wondered whether Miss Goddard would miss the book, a collection of essays which coalesce around Bertrand Russell's unbelief, written in Russell's uncluttered classicist style. I liked *Why I am not a Christian* a lot, but Voltaire's *Candide* which I read around the same time did a lot to advance me further in the direction of doubt and scepticism. Miss Goddard later became the germ for a short story I wrote long ago.

My uncle, Mother's brother, Mr M Akin-Olotu, had the largest collection of books in their hometown of Ifon. When he retired as Director of News and Current Affairs in the state's radio station, he went back to Ifon. I didn't know he had so many books until he came back home. At the time I was being cock-a-hoop about Ms Goddard's books, I wasn't aware that my own uncle had almost as many in the attic of his house. During my university days, whenever I visited him in Ifon, I always borrowed one book or the other, or several at a time. The library shelves were weighed down with 'Completed Works': Shakespeare, August Strindberg, Henrik Ibsen, Dickens, Oscar Wilde, George Bernard Shaw, CS Lewis and others. Beyond being gripped by powerful naturalistic plays written by the Scandinavians, the canny cleverness of Oscar Wilde and the gladiatorial wit George Bernard Shaw kept me returning to their works again and again. Collected in a huge hardback, I polished off the whole works of Wilde in a few days. But there were these little Penguin editions of Shaw's plays which kept turning up on the shelves of the library, just as I thought I had read the last, another would emerge, buried between some other identical Penguin books. When I read the title *The Adventures of the Black Girl in Search of God* on the spine of a book, with Shaw's name as author, I was somewhat surprised, because even though I had not read all of Shaw's plays, I knew all the titles by heart.

Black Girl in Search of God is not a play, it is prose, fiction, a lengthy story of an African girl who has just become a Christian and has taken the injunction 'Seek and you shall find me' in earnest. The black girl quests after God, physically, like a determined and overambitious Old Testament prophet might do. As she progresses, this pragmatic pilgrim meets figures from the family tree of Abraham, she argues with them, clobbers them with both logic and a knobkerrie. After a detour into domesticity, marrying a flame-haired Irishman and raising children, the black girl continues her quest. This Shavian allegory was ahead of its time when it was written and it is still ahead of its time today. True, African girls now go out in search of God in huge numbers, but it is far less likely that they would hold a knobkerrie and do a lot of arguing on the way. The story had at first brought me in the mind of Miss Goddard, although being an atheist she had not been going round looking for God. Or had she? Wasn't art her god, and the Artist a priest at the shrine of art, African art? I imagine the name 'Goddard' also contributed to the association of the Englishwoman with the story of the black girl looking for her God. And there was Suzanne Wenger, the Austrian woman who arrived in the art-sodden town of Osogbo some 60 years ago. Wenger made the place her home, made the traditional religion her own, became the Chief Priestess and Custodian of the shrine of the river Osun Goddess, built a house, which became a fastness for traditional African beliefs. Wenger grew a thick skin against the aspersions and animus of local Christians and Muslims. I wrote *The Adventures of Two White Girls in*

Search of Their Gods not so much as a spoof of Shaw's story but as a way of saying 'it takes all sorts'.

I was no longer looking for any god, or indeed God, when I wrote the story. My search, if I ever had any, had ended several years before. I no longer 'believed,' I had become a lapsed Anglican, if I was ever a signed-up Anglican in the first place. If my baptismal certificate indicates that I was once a rubricated Anglican, the seal was only accepted by proxy, by parental prerogative.

I also remember reading Samuel Butler's *The Way of All Flesh* as a young man, a couple of years after I no longer saw myself as a Christian. But whenever I look back at how I decided to turn back from the overbeaten and dusty road of belief, of faith-without-evidence, to the less-trodden if also foggy path of secular reasonableness, I always remember the main character of the book, Ernest Pontifex – Pontifex goes to prison a curate and comes out a sceptic.

The only thing close to an institution in which I was an inmate was a university, and this certainly was no prison, in spite of often coming across as a formulaic, compartmentalizing crammer where you were expected to regurgitate what your teachers had regurgitated earlier, a place you went to cramp rather than nurture your style. As early as Year One, in the space for Subject on the cover of a notebook, I had written *Prison Notes*. It was not altogether a conscious conclusion, I wasn't feeling incarcerated, I wasn't feeling choked or coffined, but when I wrote those words, I had become a compulsive doodler, a squiggler for its own sake. If I was chatting with a friend, for instance, and I had anything that looked like paper before me, all I needed was a pen or pencil before I began to disfeature it with bits of written stuff, desultory notations, two or three words in the course of an hour's chat, a name of someone mentioned, a word spoken or even unspoken. The doodling would be done so undeliberately and unobtrusively that the friend might not even notice, even though the word or words might be traced and retraced over and again until it would become vividly calligraphed yet pointless. *Prison Notes* may have been written in these circumstances, spin-off of mere automatism, rather than the result of a protest against the university system. But then, as a depth psychology geek, I may not be too eager to wish away any visceral interpretation of the words *Prison Notes*. I might just as well have seen a university as a prison, a stifling stuffy purgatory palled over by the sober soaraway wings of academic gowns, paled about by the steel rods of instructionism and sameness, where everyone is shoehorned into a sedentary capsule. Doesn't the French thinker, Michel Foucault, bracket the university, the school, with the prison in his power/control/enclosure continuum? Actually, the university I attended – though it was what might be called a 'second generation' institution, similar to the British redbrick – was not a bad place to study. I spent a lot of time in the Student Union Buttery drinking beer and smoking cigarettes – mere poseur puffing, really – with friends. Tuition was all right, and there was nothing stifling about being a student in the institution, or if it was so I didn't notice as I spent a chunk of my time reading extracurricularly, looking forward to when I would go 'home' again and browse through titles in my uncle's library.

I knew there was religion around, on the campus, but the student religionists went about their business with little fuss: no invasive preachings, no overt overloud song-and-dance about belief, there was a general atmosphere of go-as-you-please. There were the so-called cults too, brutalised underground incarnation of fraternities and societies. Although to belong in any of the cults was to be seen as a member of one of the campus streetwise cliques, all I heard were only tales of murders, of rapes, of initiation hazing gone wrong. And there was the Palmwine Drinkards Club, a club whose libational and dionysian bacchanalia I liked to watch from the sidelines but was not interested in joining. There was nothing like a secular/atheist club, and even if I thought about it I could not have taken the initiative. Because even in a Nigerian university in those last decades of the 20th century, belief in God and the sovereign necessity of religion were absolute and inexpungeable, and to think of starting anything like an atheist club would be gravely counterintuitive.

Throughout my undergraduate days I lived in a bedsitter in an off-campus tenement, and about a dozen other university students also lived in the sprawling house. Three of the student tenants were studying philosophy, but for much of the time chats among the male students often drifted towards politics, money and how to 'make it', towards girls and every sort of lubricious gossip. One day I barged into one of the rooms of the boys reading philosophy, he was discussing Nietzsche with his two course mates. Although I was in the English department, I had been loosely interested in some of the things happening in the philosophy class of my year since I got into university. I did an 'Introduction to Philosophy' course in Year One and I had made a couple of friends in the class, both of whom were often pleasantly puzzled by my interest in some of their more argument-based topics. In Year Three I joined them again for a political philosophy lesson: Rousseau, Machiavelli, Hobbes, Marx – I remember that I read Marx's 'religion as opiate' in clearer, fuller context, although all I had read about the Soviet Union told me the road to Marx's good intentions might turn out to be pretty hellish. If I knew when the class treated the atheological aspects of religion, I would have been interested in the class and would have taken the subject as an elective – but such a course was never part of the curriculum. The nearest I got to discussing belief and the lack of it with any student was when I went to the shared rooms of two of the philosophy students. I had just been reading Nietzsche's *Thus Spake Zarathustra* and I could not but bring it up. I enthused that *Zarathustra* had some most sublime passages that I had ever read and that Nietzsche might as well turn out to be my favourite philosopher. One of the guys said: 'Because he said God is dead? Ade, I know you do not quite believe in God. You would like Nietzsche, of course.'

'Well, you know there is more to Nietzsche's pronouncement that God is dead. He put it in the mouth of the madman most of the time anyway.'

'You know what the Bible says about the mad man, that he believes in his heart that there is no God. Look at Nietzsche himself, he dared say there is no God, that God is dead. What happened to him? He went mad. That should serve as a lesson for all budding Nietzsches.'

I also missed such a topic as Theodicy or The Problem of Evil in the philosophy class (if it was ever taken), but I selected an analogous elective in the Theology Department in my Third Year. It was about God, the attributes of God, the ontology of God, if that would not be considered a tautology by diehard solifidians, because to them God himself is *the* being, omnibeing. I remember that I immensely enjoyed the 'God' class because, although it was likely that the lecturer was a believer in God, his treatment of the subject was balanced and brilliant. For every positive attribute he mentioned in connection with God, he did not neglect to discuss the objections raised by sceptics. Whence evil if God is all good? Granted that God is present everywhere, does he show as much interest in what is going on inside a termitary as in the palace of Queen Elizabeth, for instance? The lecturer then spent time on St Aquinas' *apologia* for God's seeming insouciance, borrowing a leaf from the Gnostics, and using the shaky hypotheses of the Remote God (Deus Remotus, via certain traditional African religions), the Otiose God (Deus Otiosus, via Deism) and the Absconded God (Deus Absconditus, via Thomas Aquinas). Although dated and scholiastically fusty, this was a most sensible description of God, it was pretty much damning God with faint praise, and this was the way I saw the God for a few years: distant, passive and standoffish. In a short story I wrote about the death of a dictator, I used all these terms to describe the stages of the Dictator's passage. First he becomes otiose, then remote, then he absconds from public life as he lies dying, but this means that the Dictator still exists, so I decided to call the short chapter in which he exits 'Deus Absentia', the Absent God.

Which brings me to Dostoevsky. I never imagined that Dostoevsky could contribute anything to my journey into religious *disbelief*, knowing his well-recycled, overdrawn gnome of 'if you don't believe in God you will believe in anything', or is it 'anything will be possible if there is no God'? (As it happens, before I became a sure-footed questioner of religious certainties, I once described myself as an 'anythingarian' when I stumbled on the word, which, curiously enough, gave some truth to Dostoevsky's declamation. But this was only a definitional, paltry 'truth', because even if I called myself an 'anythingarian' I did not just do 'anything': I did not kill, I did not rape, I did not become a thief, I was just the person I was, a human, susceptible of lying and some youthful premarital shenanigans and peccadilloes). But the moral universe, the angst, the pithy pathos-less self-loathing, that I discovered in Dostoevsky's *Notes from Underground*, which I read first of all his works, had made me begin a quest for the other books of the great Russian writer. During some of my serendipitous discoveries of books amongst the dust, dirt and the ruck of merchandise in the street markets of Lagos, I was able to pick up *Crime and Punishment*, *The Idiot*, *The Possessed*, all within a couple of days of each other (I found the five-volume Leon Edel's biography of Henry James the same way). I devoured the books like an obsessively driven bibliophage in any Dostoevsky's book. But even before I found the books I knew that *The Brothers Karamazov* would be *the* big find, the big read. This might appear quirky and melodramatic to anyone who did not know that even in my teenage years, churches and shacks which passed for churches, had beaten the number of libraries in any Nigerian city by a thousand to one. In other words, while a city of about 100,000 might harbour about 1,000 churches, only one library would cater to the needs of those who knew of its existence and had the time and desire to visit it. So there was nothing exactly quixotic about looking for a title in the streets of Lagos for months and even years without finding it. Such was my urge to read the renowned Grand-Inquisitor passage of *The Brothers Karamazov* that when I couldn't find it I wrote a short story about a young man who is doing a similar thing as I was, questing after *Karamazov*, but in the story the young man finds the book but loses it before he can read a single page of it. I read *Karamazov* about a decade later when I bought it in a bookshop in Banjul, Gambia, and truly, the Grand Inquisitor pullout remains memorable.

Apart from seeing heaven and hell as a curious yarn, in the long run a confluence of things had at last made me a doubter. Before Nietzsche, there was Thomas Paine, and Voltaire, and Russell and dozens other authors and books. But then book-reading cannot simply be the reason I began to re-evaluate my belief in God, or in prayer, and to see religion for what it is: balsam for those who need it – and a lot of people do need it – *maya,* illusion. Actually during the careering transition to what I may call committed agnostic – heavily leaning towards atheism (ultimately, I would call myself an apatheist) – I still prayed once in a while and the more I did it the more I realised the uselessness of what I was doing, the silly dissipation of the little time I had to do whatever else I wanted to do. And there was this evangelical church I attended two consecutive Sundays, whose pastor was so slick and 'spivvy' – this dated slang describes him better – and whose wife was so conspicuously resplendent, that I had to ask myself during the second attendance what I was doing there.

What I was doing was to see if there was a pretty girl who might beam at the flick of my torch. This might be bad faith, fleshly hypocrisy if you will, but then I would only feel any compunction, or even a twinge of conscience, if I were genuinely religious – a male animal following the scent of a female animal is as fundamentally Darwinian as foraging for food when hungry, I tried to justify myself. As a matter of fact, one of the reasons I turned away from religion was the ludicrousness of waiting until 30 or 40 or whenever I decided to get married (I wonder what would happen if I decided not to) before I would do anything in a sexual way, and I was also expected to do without the relief and pleasures of onanism. Even as a boy I never had any feeling of guilt about self-gratifying 'aberrations' I indulged in, nor did I think it was anything worthy of contrition or confession – well, except in an augustly crass Portnoyesque sense. And in my adolescent head I thought a church, a trendy evangelical church, would be a good place to seduce semi-pious 'spares,' to insinuate myself into the assailable sin-prone vessels of pretty middle-class girls with pretensions of faith.

Apart from trying to win a girl, I was also curious about how things were done in the growing, arriviste evangelical churches but, unfortunately, I had chosen a church whose presiding couple were outstandingly extrapolative of the incipient happy-clappy evangelical culture and whose method was a barbarisation of Nietzsche's improbable, self-teasing call to devotional song-and-dance. I realised that though there was a good number of pretty girls to be seen, they were so full of the New Christianity of the Pentecostals and its charismatic mannerisms and jargon that I thought it would be a waste of my time and theirs if I went beyond swapping difficult cheesy grins and partaking of end-of-service handlinking. Having not long discovered W B Yeats, via his beautiful poem, *Long-Legged Fly*, I found that instead of listening to the truly mellifluous voice of the pastor, I was reciting to myself the lines: *That girls at puberty may find the first Adam in their thought, shut the door of the Pope's Chapel, keep those children out...* Drawing on a merry cocktail of Yeats, the church girls, and Madam Muse, I wrote *Long-Legged Lass*, a bawdy song which has no place in this book.

I did indeed 'woo' and later went out with a girl who was a member of one of the numerous evangelical churches mushrooming at the time. We were about the same age – 20 – when I met her and she was a student of secretarial studies at a polytechnic. At first she couldn't believe anyone could be as casually uninterested in religion as I was, but I think she liked me and might have thought she would be able to lead me back to the fold. After a couple of years of what some of the more rigidly prudish members of her church might describe as 'sinfulness' or overexposure to carnal knowledge, my born-again girlfriend wrote a letter to me. In the epistle, she repeated how much she loved me, how much she would love to be with me for the rest of her life, that she had never met anyone like me and so on. But then she had to leave me to pursue my interests, she'd rather be alone in a room, chaste and pure, reading her Bible and communing with God than spending time to help type my stories and poems, some of which are so positively sinful they writhed with the serpents of carnality. More than all, she would leave me to my irreligion, because I had led her somewhat astray from the straight and righteous path – although this was not entirely my fault as she loved me enough to even consider giving up her faith and her love for Jesus. But she now only wanted to practise her Christianity better, and when she graduated from polytechnic a few months later she would like to meet a born-again person like her – she then wished me the best of luck. I could only wish her better luck too, she was the sweetest human being I had ever met, something that had less to do with her Christianity than with her innate good nature. I took everything with un-Christian good grace, I wasn't sure the relationship, which distance had compromised, was going anywhere anyway, and I was relatively young, 22 or 23. And if Miss Q was feeling guilty about our relationship, I couldn't see why she should not cut herself off. I hoped she knew me well enough to be certain that I would plump for her happiness first – not before mine, of course, but before any companionable joy and carnal ecstasy that I may have had in being with her. There was also the realisation that if I did not reborn myself as a Christian and if she did not de-Christianise (she would never do that) or at least water down her beliefs (no chance of that, either), we would, with time, drift apart anyway. I indeed hoped she would find what she was seeking in the born-again man she would finally settle for, a man who would not suddenly blurt out 'Holy Shit!' when he was in her presence. Because the last we saw each other, I had said those words in a fit of some kind of excitation. For the first time Miss Q admonished me. When I look back now at how it ended between me and Miss Q, I knew the creedal causativeness of the split may have given a lift to my decision to completely relieve myself of the deadweight of religion and its reliquary.

The workings of the mind are so complex and probably as mysterious as the well-theologised Mind of God that there is no way I can write with any specificity about how I reached solid sceptical conclusions about religion and God. A composite picture of realities, truths, deductions, abductions and non-sequiturs would have gathered in my mind. The seeming randomness of everything. The silence, even muteness, of God (always assuming he is somewhere). The plausibility of evolutionary Darwinism against the mythical monogenism of Adam and Eve. The Problem of Evil. Hamartiology (The Study of Sin). The hot air that is Negative Theology. The Trilemma of Trinity (and the ridiculousness of Lewis' Trilemma which proposes that Jesus could either be a lunatic, a liar or *the* lord, and since he could not be the first two he was the last!). Plus I found I could get by without God, that I did not need God, or religion, to tell me what is wrong or right just as I would not have needed him or his commandments when I was an infant to tell me what was big or small – a bit of common sense would have done that for me. And I realised one does not need God or gods to crystallise morality, to act as moral whiphand. I neither need religion as anchorage nor as moorings. After I had cut the painter, I saw with cool clear-sightedness the irrelevance of religion or God to the motions of my personal boat – and everything about that boat, a single-seat kayak, say, whether it sails fine, shimmies, tilts, spins, flounders, overturns, is in the hand of inanimate but capricious nature.

While the loss of my big sister was significant in the apotheosis of my scepticism, it is only incidental to my atheological *summa*. Of course, who knows how the mind would dispose itself in other circumstances? There is no way of surmising what might, or might not, have happened if I had not lost my sister when I was 18, a crucial and impressionable waypoint. Even if my mind had begun to lean on the side of doubt and disbelief, an inexplicable sea change might yet have happened somewhere within the labyrinths of being, something that might bring me back to religion with a vengeance.

The burial service for Mojisola was held at St Andrew's Anglican, the church in whose choir she sang, the church in which she – and all of her brothers and sisters – were baptised, where she was confirmed as a Christian. Following after Mother and Father, Mojisola was also a teacher in St Andrew's Primary, the school we all attended. When Mojisola went to join the evangelical church it was as if she had committed a quasi-religious aberration, a detour which turned out to be the 'proximate cause' of her death. But it was only too natural that her funeral service would be held at St Andrew's Anglican Cathedral. It was late afternoon, vespers hour. I can recall it all, the sombre air which mantled everything: the processional, the service, the recessional. I remember being stumped, during the service, by the following: *'I am the resurrection and the life. He who believes in me will live, even though he dies,' says the Lord (John 11:25).*

In spite of this unctuous piece of placebo, I actually began to believe less in Him.

Portrait of My Dead Brother

I do not know whether I would have been interested in art when growing up if I didn't have a brother who is a talented artist. I remember how Akin and I, as teenagers, imagined we were cognoscenti of the works of Picasso, Braque and other cubists. And of the works of neo-impressionists. I liked Van Gogh as much as Akin did; we both saw the narrative picture in which Van Gogh tells his own story through his letters to his brother, Theo. But of all the artists we talked about, Dali was the one whose physiognomy Akin seemed to be hugely interested in. He reproduced images of Dali's face a lot of times, often with pencil, drawling out the mustachio with flair and humour. I think it was Dali's curlicued moustache which attracted Akin to the face of the Spanish artist. Sometimes he would draw the mustachio without putting a face to it. In one crayonwork, he reproduced the poster of Alfred Hitchcock's *Birds*, the birds were many Dali mustachios mounted on snarling snorting mouths.

I once bought a book about Dali in Lagos. It tells the story of the artist and carries many of his works. It was in the book that I first saw the picture captioned *Portrait of My Dead Brother*. Like most of Dali's works, this is avant-garde, a prefigurement of pop-art. The face of a young boy, Benday-dotted in light and shade with cherries, a merging of Dali's faced and that of a brother who died before he was born, also called Salvador Dali. The apparition of a bird – a crow, maybe (someone said it is a vulture) – shades over the boy's brow like an oversized naevus. Among the figures in the pastiche are the couple from Millet's *Angelus* praying over what is believed to be their dead child transposed into potatoes in Millet's final version. It is one of the more sober works of the flamboyant and brazenly tricksy Dali, and I had only glanced over it in the book. I was more interested in his more colourful curiosa.

When I lost my brother Femi to cancer, the picture had come back, not directly though. I was talking to Akin – who came after Femi – on the phone, co-remembering Femi and how it was unfortunate and sad that we had to lose him, and Dali's picture had returned to me with eidetic clarity. I will leave the reason the picture came back to neuroscientists to theorise over, because the remembrance of Femi himself, his human, living form, was more powerful, more compelling, his philosophic mien, the quiet untroubled tenor of his voice – a reflection of his equipoise, his spiritual and moral largesse. How could he go, just like that?

I will go back to late 2000. I was working in the Gambia as journalist as a freelance writer, and later during that year I joined The Gambian Observer as a staff writer. Months into the job, I was made Arts and Books Editor. I had a column in the newspaper that I called 'Liferature', the upshot of an infatuation with 'portmanteau' words and equivoques. My first article for the newspaper as a freelance writer was entitled 'Millennium Smog', an attempt to navigate the smoke, fug and fog, enveloping the Millennium Bug ballyhoo. Liferature, as I discursively explained in my column after I came up with the word, was about Life and Literature, or life seen through the panoramic prism of literary consciousness, from a liberal-artistic vantage point, everything from a skit about boy wooing a girl to having one ear for rap music and the other for baroque/classical music. I also wrote an obituary of a friend and colleague who died when he was in his late 40s.

Before the war Dr Tumoe used to be a lecturer at Fourah Bay University, Freetown, Sierra Leone. He was an exile in the Gambia when I was working for The Observer, he proofread the paper. We used to discuss a lot of literature and books; I remember that he considered my interest in the works of George Bernard Shaw quaint and curious for someone who also liked Harold Pinter and his works, he also dismissed Shaw as *passé*. I told Tumoe that if both men had written at about the same time, the difference between them might not be that stark, except that one might be seen as wisely loquacious and the other profoundly terse. Although I knew the cause of his death, my conclusion in the article was that, in a transcendent sense, Tumoe died of heartbreak, the traumatic experience of being uprooted suddenly by the war from his home country. If Tumoe, a believer in God, could read an article I wrote months after his abruption, I wonder what he would have made of it. It was entitled *God is an African,* the piece was a straightforward censure of the attitude of Africans to religion. I imagine the late Sierra Leonean, ever the gentleman, would be more understanding than some of those who read and reacted to it.

The Gambia is not populated by bearded fatwaing mullahs and Islamic theocrats lording it over a cowed population with circumscribing Koranic diktats. The country is ruled by a military-despot-turned-civilian-autocrat who converted from Christianity, a minority religion, to Islam. The togaed president makes no bones about being keenly Islamic, apostolically Islamic, he even carries a sword around, tucked immodestly under his white robes (although the president describes himself as a witch-hunter and catcher, besides being an AIDS-curer – a sorcerer of sorts). But in spite of the Levantine posturing of the Allah-bothering president, the thousands of imams and marabouts the country has, and the fact that almost the whole of the population would consider themselves Muslim, it is a reasonably open society, religiously open. But it is open in so far as the remaining population who is not Muslim belongs to a religion like Christianity, and any of the expatriates who live in the country can also get on with being a closet Buddhist or crocodile-worshipper if they like...

But like in most African societies, irreligiousness is unfashionable in the Gambia, godlessness is not only morally wrong, it is also existentially anomalous, you just cannot strut around pronouncing belief in nothing. My unconventional outlook about God, the idea of God, and religion, finally cost me my position on the newspaper. The managing director, a career philanderer who always wore traditional barrel-sleeved kaftans, concluded that since I did not believe in God and since I only wrote from a secular-infidel angle, an angle further sharpened and animated with a kind of freewheeling parajournalistic style, I must certainly be writing for a certain Mr. Devil. It did not help that I was not a Gambian, for all he cared I might as well have been forged in the crucible of hell.

After I left The Observer, I decided to visit Britain, to cool off. My brother, Dupe, the first child of the family, had been living in the country for two decades. I arrived on a cold early-April morning in 2001, jaded and dozy. I thought it could not have been jetlag, there was only one hour difference of time, so no vast time zone had been passed. My brother had gone to work, but his wife and children were home and I fell asleep on the sofa for hours and only stirred when my Dupe returned. That was when he broke the news: Femi had died in Nigeria, he succumbed to *the* cancer. I was bleary-eyed from sleep, addled with tiredness, and the bad news hadn't helped. I began to grieve properly hours later when I started to accept that I would not see my brother again, because that is the simple point of death: disappearance, immaterialisation of memory – nothing remains but fond remembrances, or dreams, if anyone was lucky, or unlucky, to have them.

It wasn't exactly an unexpected death. Femi had been ill for months. Before I left the Gambia I had begun to reconcile myself to the inevitability of the pendent loss. Femi had throat cancer and the prognosis was poor. Unknown to me, he died while I was inside the plane winging its way towards England. Of course there was no such thing as a sign: no crow had soared high enough to slap its wings against the window of the plane close to where I sat, Femi's spectre had not come into the plane to whisper to me that he had passed, and no telling sibylline dreams had intruded on the short naps that I had. I was snug in the unusually comfortable seat of the plane for much of the time, reading a compact and sparely written novel entitled *Einstein's Dreams* and following the plane's trajectory on a plasma screen as it nosed its way towards England.

A week after I arrived in England I sent a semi-lament about Femi's death to the Gambian newspaper, a rather short-winded article reflecting the state of my mind. I wrote about reading the novel *Einstein's Dreams*, about grappling with relativity, dimensions, space and time, flight, and my arrival in England, being hit with the news of Femi's death – and the dream that I had. Because in spite of myself, I had indeed dreamt. At first, briefly I had seen my brother jogging down a rather Dickensian London street alongside the late dreadlocked Zimbabwean writer, Dambudzo Marechera. It was dank, dark and shadowy, and the writer, a creative genius, was puffing away at a cigarette. I remember telling myself even in the dream that Femi and Marechera had nothing in common. My brother had little interest in literature, he was the most numerate of us siblings, for him maths was a cakewalk, he even went to a technical college, read mechanical engineering. But he didn't run with Marechera for long before I found myself trotting alongside the troubled writer, and I had asked the dead Zimbabwean: why are you smoking while running? *To fucking keep the cold out*. Then I found myself in a fluorescent-lit large lounge, the place was empty, save for an old typewriter placed in the centre of a table, which was in its turn placed in the centre of the room. While I looked at the typewriter wondering what it was doing there, Marechera said: *I've got to go now, the shits will be gunning for me soon.* He was gone, and I woke up.

This was by all means a strange dream, which is what dreams are most of the time – strange and quirky. A Nigerian friend who was still working as a journalist in the Gambia offered a sweet interpretation in the way of Marechera metaphorically passing on his typewriter to me and all that, and I could just abstract my brother from the dream, make a Virgil/Dante-stroll-through-the-Circles-of-Hell out of it. But then the interpretation might be less involved than it seemed. I had been interested in Marechera as an artist for some time, something not uncommon for 'African' writers of my generation. Even when I was living in the Gambia, I had thought of writing a play, a duologue, featuring Marechera and a younger Nigerian writer. When I arrived in the UK, some of the earlier books that I borrowed from Lewisham library and read were by Marechera, and in one of his stories he wrote about a Nigerian in a vivid and memorable way – this could easily have brought on the dream. And among Marechera mavens, it is common knowledge that he once pawned his typewriter to feed his habit of drug-taking and drinking, so the typewriter I saw in the dream might be an oblique remembrance of the one the troubled writer pawned. My brother may have been part of the dream because he had just died and my mind had been fairly exercised by his loss. The dream may have been the result of a conjuncture of things conscious and unconscious. But then again, a few days after I had the dream, another had supervened, a strange and eerie dream, not so manifestly connected to my late brother, except if one wishes to use Jungian metaphysics in its interpretation.

As dreams go, this was a long one. When I read somewhere that it is possible for a dream to play itself out episodically, I didn't think much of it until I had this one. With a rare and dramatic persistence, the dream, which may have begun around three in the morning, chugged to a finish at six when I finally woke up fully. Many years before, when Akin and I went to hometown with Father, a boy – his name was Dada – told us a story about how he lost the dreadlocks he was born with. It was this story that was retold in the dream, rather disembodiedly, because a voice which sounded like Femi's commentated on the images I was seeing. I have reproduced the dream here as best as I can, although it is considerably drawn out and stylised for literary purposes.

*

I was a special child – as special as an *abiku* child who returned again and again to his parents. But I was not that kind of revenant. Even when I was born *abiku*, like many superstitious absurdities and prodigies, were becoming extinct, they were being stared down by a braver newer world. But one of the things that made me a special child was that I, like the *abiku*, had manifestly returned to earth, not just 'born' like other ordinary babies. My return was by no means an exercise in weird mischievous flirtation with *being, time* and *nothingness* as in the case of an *abiku*, it is more than that, more meaningful. For only a couple of hours after my paternal great-grandfather died, I was delivered into the world with a ready heaven-sent name of Babatunde, *Father has returned to us*.

I like this thing about bespoke names. No one was supposed to know the name of a baby until the seventh day when he was given a name by a priest, so to have one from the womb was a privilege. A child who came out foot first had his pluperfect name too, *Ige*, a jokey epithet translatable into *A stubborn calf kicking over the traces*. But the diehard *abiku* was the favourite of the gods, coddled by parents, treated like a godling upon whose head palm oil, nut oil, olive oil and every sort of emollient must be poured, more than all there was always the oleaginous overlay of awe to the parental pampering. Since I was not an *abiku*, awe had transposed into reverence in my case, being a reincarnate great-grandfather. And like an ancient, I was born bald, for my great-grandfather had gone plain glabrous by the time he died.

Like any number of babies born bald, hair began to grow on my scalp after a few weeks, but as if to remind everyone of my specialness, the hair had burgeoned into stud-like ravelled knots. My hair protested the vanity of the soft curliness of baby hair with its scrubby growth, which was neither combable nor brushable. Thorough brushing had endeavoured to fine down pieces of the tough weed of hair, but often before the brush was out of it, tuftlets of hair would reach curlingly for each other with wry magnetism, static electricity crackling. There was power in my hair, it was concluded, in my head, and the head being the seat of not only the mind but also of the soul, of self, of being and spirit, I was given a closer watch… Signs, signs of significance and difference, of uniqueness – like a child born with a tooth or two in place, from whose mouth wise words, truths, blessings and maledictions would issue, a child whose precocious verbal ability should be feared. My knotty hair might as well be a foreordination of a head that would wear a crown.

It turned out a few weeks later that I was a Dada, a child who grew solid coalesced hanks of hair, dreadlocks, locks you could neither comb nor brush. The impact this had on my grandfather was considerable, the awe of me being his father had aggrandised into overawe. My hair was sprouting dreadlocks all right, but the issues here were fundamentally different from mere Rastafarianism. Rastafarians, in their quest for mysticism that wore the colour of identity, of protest, had decided to leave their hair uncombed, snarled, the hair growing in lush locks. But to be born with the beginnings of dreadlocks like me was to belong to the gods – particularly to a certain gargantuan dreadlocked god who was said to come down to earth from its home somewhere in the heavens, galloping through the world shrouded in a pillar of wild whirlwind. When my folks saw that I was beginning to sprout the magical locks, they knew that I belonged to the god.

Grandfather took me to a priest who could commune with gods. The priest told the old man that the god of dreadlocked children and whirlwind had confirmed what he often told parents: a dreadlocked child belonged to him, the god, so the child must always be treated as a little god. The child must not be smacked, must not be told off, whatever wrong he did, he must always be pampered. Even if he slapped his mother he must be spared, even if he cursed at his father he must not be touched, even if he kicked the head of his sleeping older sibling he must be petted, even if he became unruly and destructive he should be serenaded with personal praise-song, he should be exempt from every reprimand, and every year a red-plumed cock should be offered as a sacrifice to him and the god.

Although my great-grandfather lived to be 100-odd, his son believed he had gone away only to make a place for me, or had gone in order to return as me. I never saw the picture of the patriarch who had returned as me, somehow no one had thought of taking a photograph of him. Anyway, it was passed down to me that I looked like him. This ancestor was a farmer who was also a journeyman voodooist, but significantly he was a healer who knew a thing or two about herbs – people went to him with minor ailments like headaches and fevers and he would give them a combination of herbs to decoct. Years before I was born, he was said to have predicted that my father, one of his many grandchildren, would have a child who would turn out to be him.

When I was a boy I prided myself on being a special child. I was my great-grandfather as well as being the offspring of the whirlwind god. The priest my grandfather took me to also buttressed my superbeing status when he pronounced that the god did not say when the dreadlocks would be cut. This was very important. Only a favoured Dada enjoyed this sort of silence from the god. The oracular deity often revealed to his priests the age a child's dreadlocks would be cut – usually not more than nine years. It was one of the mysteries of Dadahead that after the locks had been cut ceremonially, normal hair would grow in their place and after that the child would remain the whirlwind god's child by name only: Dada. The god had no use for grown-ups, so usually by age 9 every child with dreadlocks would have had them shaved off, often several years before he was nine. But it seemed the god wanted me to be his lapdog for more than nine years, he was silent about the haircut. I was a sacred cow, or if one were to be accurate about these things, I was a sacred calf – I even feel even compelled to describe myself as a sacred baboon. To the ancient Egyptians, baboons were sacred, just like cows to the Hindu, especially the dog-faced male baboon which sports a long silver mane.

When I was a child, relatives worshipped me, women of the house fought to carry me in their arms, rub me against their bosoms and their womb, because a Dada was believed to be the bringer of fertility. Even if a woman who was pronounced barren had faith in the Dada, she might come to have as many children as the locks on the head of the child. Often I ate from the same plate as Grandfather, something that was, without irony, a big deal. I could see easily that I was the personification of a portent, and I found it charming to be lovely and cuddlesome one minute, wicked and difficult the next. I strutted on the turf of my free-agency, dispensing doses of gall and syrup all around. Although it was certain that my request would be granted, I screeched like a sacred baboon whenever I needed anything. I was my grandfather's father, and I was reminded of this both in words and deeds. More than all, I was the favourite of the whirlwind god who gave me my special hair.

My locks grew fast. By the time I was four they had dropped as far my shoulders, gorgeous-looking and all thread-straight, with only a few decorative crotches and reticulations. There were salient filaments of grey fretted within many of the black locks, like you might see on the head of a dreadlocked elderly man, but on my infant head the effect was stately and uncanny, it must have added to the stuporous awe in which my being was held. The great-grandfather in me had manifested in the locks, they were like a crown on my head, and only a few would dare touch them even if I allowed them. I often almost screamed my head off whenever they were touched deliberately – rarely, a great dare – or by accident. The god of whirlwind was a profoundly feared deity and the hair of his godson was sacrosanct. The locks were shampooed at the whim of my petulance and temperament. Sometimes for months I would not allow Grandmother, or anyone, to bring water near it. A swarming attack of lice, mites, and the grave discomfort they brought made me succumb to occasional washing of the hair. And during such shampooing I would become shirty, making the whole process pretty thumby for the normally efficient hands of Grandmother. I always felt better though after the washing. I wonder where the myth that lice and Dada locks were compatible came from, that their relationship was symbiotic and happy, the locks growing longer and lusher and the lice helping to cleanse them by feeding on the accretion of grease and grime in the locks. I had no doubt that the lice were sucking more blood than grime, my scalp was always itchy – before the wash.

When I was six, I began primary school and I carried into the school not so much my princely spleen as a sort of pomposity. I was one of two dreadlocked children in the school. When I was in the first year the other child, a girl, was in year three. She was a shy child and I knew, perhaps by Dada instinct, that the girl's locks would soon be cut.

At school, my locks fairly long, I enjoyed a lot of immunity. No pupil would dare beat a Dada for fear the whirlwind spirit would punish him by carrying him away to his abode in the clouds for seven years, using him as his servant. I did not know whether my early teachers – luckily all women – believed this thing about the spirit carrying anybody away for seven years, but the female teachers always did not touch me even on occasions when they had to cane everyone in the class. The only punishment they could bring themselves to give was telling me to raise my hands above my heads and close my eyes, and never with the normal complement of kneeling. The teachers, I thought, did not wish to be scourged with childlessness – or bereavement, for those who had children. Often all a woman teacher could do was sigh and say soppily, 'You, this Dada boy, don't you be troublesome now', or any such lame and inane admonition.

I was really not a bad boy at school, it was as if my guardian god had intervened to moderate my excesses. I did not screech, or whinny, or purr as frequently as I did at home, all I did was harmless pupil play. But a male teacher once caned me – first time in my life – he'd caught me making a rich racket with my classmates when our mistress was not in the class and he was teaching the next class on the block. Just as he gave other boys, he gave me six strokes of his cane on the palm of my hand. And did I cry! I was not even sure he noticed my locks, and if he did he could not care a strand of hair. But I was certain my god, my guardian spirit, the whirlwind god, would punish the man for what he did. I also hoped for this and more when, weeks later, the headmaster made a random visit to my classroom and called me out. Closely, he examined my dreadlocks, without touching them, and I would have thought he was in awe if he was not wearing a grimace with an edge of distaste, as if the locks were roundworms struggling to find their way out of a mound of shit. Then he said: 'These things are filthy. Tell your mother to wash them always. I am sure they have lice in them. I don't know why they would not cut the dreadful things early. The god nonsense.'

I had expected the god to show instant anger, I mean *ire* of unimaginable weight. I expected the god to work in concert with his friend, Sango, the thunder-god, and strike the headmaster in the head, split the man's head and spill his brains, the horrible man who dared insult me, my sacred elflocks, I the son of a god. Nothing happened, not even the tiniest mishap, for days, weeks… I was hugely disappointed. But I had to console myself with the thought that the god had forgiven the headteacher, after all gods were supposed to combine the dual attribute of wrath and benevolence.

At school I learnt more about the whirlwind god, often by way of schoolground myths spun to my interest. He was a hairy superman. The god of whirlwind moved about skyclad, he had nothing for clothes but his flowing ankle-long dreadlocks and each shock of lock as thick as the tail of stallion, and there were several hundred of these on the head of the god, pleached, antlered, interdigitated. Down on earth, the god did not move like a walking man, he spun on a leg, the other leg held up like a stork's, and his locks would spread out as wide as a chopper's fan whenever he was spinning. When the god used both legs to spin, a whirlwind would become a terrestrial maelstrom, meaning the god was very angry, that he was in high dudgeon. In the god's wake, anyone who could pick the tiniest strand of his lock would become the richest man on earth, for this was the ultimate talisman. No one had ever been able to seize the strand, though.

More interestingly, I learnt the whirlwind god might decide to carry away a Dada with his locks, up there to his heaven's abode, an orchard planted with citrus, a thousand genera, besides orange, tangerine, clementine, mandarin… In a corner there was a huge barbecue, always laden with heavy slabs of mutton, roasting over a red-hot field of charcoal. The god loved mutton so much that this was the only thing he ate every day, a chunk as big as a big sheep, picking any number of fruits and eating them for a chaser – he didn't drink any liquid, he was a solid god. The mutton the god of dreadlocked children ate from his barbecue one day was always mysteriously replaced the next, so the grate was invariably full of browned, fat-dripping mutton. And the red smouldering fire under it was deathless. If the god took a Dada it would be a favourite one whom he would keep for three years – years of intense discipline, after which the Dada would become a powerful magician, a wonderworker. The gist of the discipline imposed on the favourite Dada was that in the years he would spend in the ethereal palace, he would only eat citrus fruits. He must not salivate for the roasting mutton, let alone nurse any hopes of tasting it. Salivation was an offence. Oversaturation of the olfactory senses with the aroma of the mutton was also punishable. A child who salivated for roast mutton would have the years he would spend in the orchard increased to seven, and if he kept salivating he would be damned never to return to earth. However, any child who returned to earth after three or seven years in the god's realm would be blessed with mysterious powers, and the returnee would remain the son and favoured one of the god for ever with the privilege of keeping his locks on head for ever, the locks becoming the cachet of demigodhood. Only a dreadlocked boy was capable of experiencing ascension, though this did not make a girl-Dada any less the offspring of the whirlwind god.

A few weeks after I began school, the girl with locks had had them cut. It was the talk among pupils, the feast and ceremonial which went with the cutting. But what interested me most about the tonsuring rites was how the girl was said to have named a billy-goat when the time came for her to name any beast or bird she wanted slaughtered for her, which she might eat alone or share with friends and family, if she wished. I wondered why the girl did not name an elephant, a buffalo, a rhino or hippo, something big and substantial and rare, she was supposed to name any beast or bird that came to her otherworldly head. I was certainly going to choose any of these big beasts – maybe a whale.

Another high point of the locks-cutting ceremonial was the sequence of strange behaviour the child who just had his locks cut often displayed. Some believed it had to do with the nicking of the crown of the head with a razor by the priest of the whirlwind god, seven blood-springing incisions on which a sort of snuff-brown powder – possibly a hallucinogenic – would be rubbed. After the incisions had been made, the child would carry on as if possessed, talking, waffling, orally wandering before he would fall into a dance, a silent but frantic dance to music that was provided by the servants of the god. This was the child's last physical dance with the god who would only have dealings with his *soul* if he still had any use for him in adulthood. After the mad dance the child would fall into a deep sleep.

The girl had her wild talk and dance after her dreadlocks were cut and then she had had her deep sleep. When I saw her at school some days later her scalp was still skinclean, the colour fairer than the rest of her body and there was a sweet symmetry to the contours of the small head that I hoped my head would mimic. Well, perhaps the god might decide to order my hair cut when I am nearing ten – the girl was about eight. The ceremonial, the feast, the dance, more than all, the meaty treat…which I was going to ask to eat alone, if only the god would want my locks cut. But I was not sure I wanted to cease being the god's favourite, this had brought on me a lot of respect: one whose locks might not be cut forever. And what couldn't I ask from my parents? They once killed several cocks for me when I said I wanted them, a goat too, a fat she-goat, though I shared everything with everyone… Being seized by the god and transported to the citrus orchard and subjected to a temptation with roast mutton was a challenge. And becoming a magician.

For three years, I was torn between whether I would like to have my locks cut and be feted and make my demand of an animal I would want killed for me, or be taken to the god's orchard in the heavens and returned after three years (I was certain I wouldn't salivate for roast mutton) to earth where I would become a magician. In my fourth year at school, my dreadlocks dropping to my waist, a magician had come to perform for us in the school hall. The man came from another town. Shortish, moustached, he wore a brown safari suit, his dreadlocks were not longer than mine, but thicker, some were cleft midway like huge tree branches and some had ends like fat fingers debouching from a chunky hand. This was the first adult I would see sporting dreadlocks. The magician stood on a makeshift wooden dais and announced to us that his name was Big Wiz, not his real name, but that was what everyone called him: his other name was Dada. Before he began performing, he gave a short speech: 'I am a natural-born Dada, I did not grow my dreadlocks like Rastafarians, these are natural Dada locks. Truly I disappeared for three years and I returned with the power to perform magic—'

During the time the magician performed, my mind was spinning like a top that won't stop, a Catherine wheel in perpetual motion, twinkling colours, light and energy and rhythm. The magician's performance, which every other child was enjoying so innocently, had become a kick-giving sideshow. I watched the magical acts with the megalomaniac eye of a poor child dreaming of a rich child's toy room. I must have this power too, I said to myself covetously, magical power to conjure out sweets, chewing gums, scarves, pigeons, kolanuts, eat and chew a mouthful of razor blades like biscuits and drink it down with Coca-Cola spirited from nowhere. When the magician left, all my classmates came round to tell me that I could become a magician too, a wonderboy. Only if I can go away for three years, I told them. To the orchard, and always assuming I didn't steal roast mutton.

For days after the magician's visit, my mind was taken with becoming a magician. I needed to go up to the orchard of the god of Dada. I had thought of how I would be swept away by the whirlwind, borne by the locks of the god himself. Of course, I saw pillars of whirlwind now and then, but people often ran from them because they carried so much dust and sand, and their strength could knock down the staunchest of men. There was also the fear that a whirlwind might *decide* to carry them to the heavens on a whim. If the whirlwind spirit carried anyone who was not a Dada away, such a person would never return, he would become an eternal servant of the god, a sort of zombie. I had no such fears, nor even any fear that I might be carried away, though sometimes I ran from the whirlwind like everyone else so as not to eat too much dust. I never believed I could be knocked down by the whirlwind, though. I would levitate, I imagined, I would become the embodiment of the ancient dichotomy of levity and gravity. In spite of the risk of becoming blinded by dust and sand I decided, firmly, to wait for the whirlwind whenever it came next…

I didn't see any for weeks, except for huge clouds of dust made by occasional vehicles speeding past. I wondered why I did not see a whirlwind for a long time. Until one late afternoon. It came, a tall geyser of dust gyrating some way down the street, spinning crabwise. It reminded me of a species of masquerader, dimensionless and without shadow, able to stand as high as three metres and flatten itself slap with the ground, its spinning motions impressive and nimble – a toysome Tower of Pisa, pirouetting. I guessed the sideways movement of the whirlwind correctly, so it slapped straight into me where I stood right in the middle of the dusty road in front of Grandfather's house. I had felt choked at first, breathless, then the uplifting had come, heavenwards.

I could not believe this would happen so easily. I had gone away in the cloud of dust right in front of everyone: the children I was playing with and Grandfather's youngest wife, she was sitting in the top balcony of the big house.

Moments later I found myself in the orchard. It was like I had imagined: hundreds of citrus trees grew in clean, beautiful, scoured earth. Paradise, here is paradise, citrus paradise, I said to myself. All around me I saw men in gowns, picking leaves off the ground as they dropped from the trees. Perhaps these were servants, everlasting servants, zombies, though they appeared more alive than the soulless undead. There were two dreadlocked white-attired men among the crop-haired lot, maybe these two were earthlings who hankered after roast mutton and were in timeless punitive purgatory. I wondered where the barbecue grate was, I'd not seen anything like it now. Fruit trees all around, citrus. I was glued to a spot, not knowing where to turn; no one seemed to have noticed me.

After a while a thin, lean man turned, slowly, to look at me for some moments, his eyes devoid of surprise. He began to walk towards me. When he was some distance from me, he crooked his finger, indicating that I follow him. Between pathless trees, I followed the man, and after some time we entered a glade, wide and swept, well-detailed like a chief's favoured square. It wasn't long before I saw the god, he was as close a figure as possible to what was in my imagination. Although he sat on what appeared like a tall great stool, a fair-sized taboret, I saw he could not be shorter than nine feet, he had lengthy limbs and long heavy prodigies of locks. I saw the eyes of the god were fire-red, his brow vast and ruckled. In the space to his left, something pulled my attention from the god: a large barbecue grate. This was the most magnificent thing a child's eye could see. My belly instinctively began to wimble – and my mouth salivated. I was hooked on the barbecue. The god began to fulminate: 'You little bellygod, you do not belong to me. You belong to earth. In your wilful mind you forced yourself upon me. I brought you up here to the heavens, to see if you were strong enough to resist the roast mutton. You have failed. You hanker after the meat. Now I must send you back to earth.' It was so summary, so snap.

Back to earth, I found myself lying face-up on a mat in what had resolved into my grandfather's large living room. Soon I discerned Grandfather sitting on his armchair, a great-uncle sat beside him on another armchair. Grandmother sat close to me on the mat waving welcome air on my half-naked body with a raffia-woven handfan. Then I saw the priest of the gods, he sat close to my head on a low wooden stool. Even as I placed everyone, my mind still half-fuddled, I heard the priest say: 'He has come back. I told you he would be back soon. Now he is awake. The spirit had entered him. That's why he behaved that way. He forced himself on the god. He must have seen the god while he was away. I have had a message from the god too. His locks will be cut tomorrow. The time is ripe. He is very tired now, he will still be tired tomorrow. Not until the locks are cut will he be himself. He is a very strong Dada. Before he goes to sleep ask him what he would like killed for him. He'll say it.'

I realised how weary I was after the priest had left. Grandmother continued to wave the fan, urging me into sleepstream. Grandfather asked what I would like to be treated with. He asked three times before I could answer, I was groggy. I wanted a she-goat. Well, it was a surprise to me later that I did not ask for a whale or a rhino, but a goat was the only thing that came to my mind, it came as if by a cue. And it was not even the god's choice meat – he was partial to ram's meat.

I slept for all of 13 hours, unbrokenly, deeply, undreamingly. Still on the mat, I had woken to the clucks of many women, coming from the courtyard of the big house. It was all too confusing, so many voices. What was I doing on the mat, had I slept there all alone, all night? Was it morning? I was not in my little bed in Grandmother's room. People came in now and then, but no one looked at me closely to see whether I had woken. My eyes were wearyingly half-open. What was going on? There were too many people around. Was there a feast today? How much had I missed? Then Grandmother came closer and saw me observing her narrowly. She said: 'Oh, I must go to tell the priest that he is awake.'

I began to make several half-baked recalls which did not hang together before the priest arrived, tying a white cloth from the waist and two ropy amulets on his upper arms. He said to me: 'Be up, my child, you will soon be relieved and be strong again.'

After he'd pulled off the stitch of underpants I wore and I stood naked, the priest led me from the sitting room to the sandy forecourt of the house. The place was swept clean. There was a stool in the middle of the open ground and a small deep calabash was placed beside the stool. The priest led me to the stool, I was as meek as bewildered Isaac being led by his father, Abraham, to the altar to be sacrificed to God. When we got to the stool the priest sat on it and told me to sit between his splayed legs. I sat, Isaac-mute. The priest brought out a clasped razor from between the knot of his wrapper and skin. Before he opened the razor he told me that in the calabash the blood of the goat I demanded had been collected, 'The locks from your hair will be mixed with the blood and both will be buried in the forest. Now let's do it.'

Before the priest began to cut the locks, a large crowd had gathered round us – a fog of faces and heads. I was getting dazed again. The cutting of the locks was neither painful nor pleasurable. I only wanted to sleep. I was sweating on the head and on my naked body. When the hair had been taken away, I felt the dewy meaty palm of the priest on my scalp, overpatting it like a novice baptiser. Then he began to incant and score my head with the razor he had used to cut the hair.

When he made the first of seven nickings he intended to make, I practically lost consciousness, the first stroke was all I remembered. I was later told how I chattered lustily, uttering deep mysteries as if I was a diviner, how I danced to no music before I ran through a rift in the crowd. They later found me where I was sleeping on my great-grandfather's gravestone in front of his ancient house. They left me to my slumber. I woke up three hours later, cool cat's paw slightly worrying the plain-favoured contours of my cropped head. Some of my relatives had lounged around while I had this last bit of sleep. When I stirred, they concentrated their gaze on me, and when they saw that I was fully awake, they came closer and picked me up.

In Grandfather's house, the feasting began, Besides the she-goat, two rams were also slaughtered, cooked, fried and stewed. I was treated like an infant crown prince who is being watched to grow up and take a vacant throne. I felt alive now, no longer tired or sleepy. Grandmother gave me a tender if thorough bath and I was dressed in new clothes. Then I melted into the spirit of the day, though a chastened deep centre in me stressed that I had lost something with the cutting of my locks, a sort of power. But then, really, it was all gone: the fear and respect I evoked at school. I was never going to become a magician. I looked forward with some regret to the day I would appear in school shorn-headed, or normal pinfeathery hair sprouting…

On the feast day some people called me Baba; some called me Dada. The names were all that remained.

*

It was not until I woke up that it occurred to me that the rather nebulous face of the dreadlocked Dada in the dream might actually be mine – or mine spliced with my brother's as in Dali's portrait. And then his seeming voice…

Was this really a dream? Naturally, I was affected by the death of my brother in a way that is not so difficult to parse. This was the second sibling that I would lose, and as the mind is not a kind of palimpsest where the first loss can be completely wiped off to give space for the other, they both registered; in spite of the intercession of time, they overlapped and conjoined. In the absence of the soporific consolation of religion, I tried to be philosophical.

However short or long the span of life one lives is, it is still a span, a bracket, I reasoned with the trite everydayness with which one can only see these things. A lifetime is invariably finite, one is bound to be a loser in the zero-sum game in which one must vacate one's earthly niche for the unknown child born at the exact moment one takes one's final leave (being born is, of course, not a gain, it is essentially a loss, however late the end is deferred). And I was conscious of the fact that the game is invariably arbitrary, unmanaged, unmediated, played on a treacherous ground. Acceptance that I would never run into my brother again was swift, but there was something about my grieving process. Well it was more of a recess, not process, or a combination of both – grieving *precess* in a manner of speaking, because whether I noticed it or not, every retrospective thought that I had, every bit of remembrance, would end in the realisation of loss, of hollowness, and the slow stodgy filling of the void with the self-consoling gruel that life feeds us.

I arrived in England on the morning of April 1st, and there was the enveloping malaise of displacement/arrival in the somewhat overcold wintry early April, *Waste Land's* cruellest month. It was for me a cruel glum month, a quietly disquiet month. It was on 1st April that I heard of the passing of my brother, which made it worse than a cruel joke, being an occasional but devout reader of TS Eliot, especially in times that I think poetry might help as a restorative. When you know someone as long as you know a brother or a sister, you often have a lot to disinter when something as tragic as a loss happens. I did not shed a single tear because my eyes had teared months before when the tumour which led to his death was becoming rampant, when I realised that there might be nothing for it but release.

So after the sad eventuation, I spent days trying to recapture the picture of Femi, his hairy arms, his fine features blending into a balding head, his soft eyes, his gentle voice, his unfussiness, our common likenesses, all the little things. And the slightly bigger ones like when Femi did what a brother often does for a brother: he stood up for me and knocked out a childhood and good friend of his in my defence. His friend, Ola, had been teasing me for some time, calling me every sort of name, making faces, taking me off, even prodding me in the back with his finger. Suddenly I had felt my gorge rise and I leant up, raised my hand, and cuffed Ola on the ear. Ola was enraged, he charged, intending to crush me. I was a gangly ten-year-old, both Ola and Femi were knocking 15, and Femi was growing up to be a strapping lad. Before Ola could reach me, Femi had stopped him with an upper-cut, and Ola just went down, curling into a foetal position. Ola's mum was one of the nicest persons I ever knew, so although she was upset that her son had to be woken up from his faint with a dash of cold water, and that the two good friends had fought, she had thought it was all not worth losing her rag over. The next day, Ola and Femi were having a laugh over the matter, although Femi had spelled it out to his friend that in future he shouldn't hit me and that if he didn't want to be slapped by a 'small boy,' he should stop bugging me. And I think that worked, because Ola never teased or worried me again.

I also recalled when Ola and Femi were seen trying to freewheel Father's Peugeot car out of our compound. Around 12.30 in the morning Father woke up by chance, came out of his room, peered through the curtains of the sitting room and saw spectral images of half a dozen people pushing his fairly new car out of the gate of the house. He opened the window fast and yelled, 'Thieves!' The apparitions faded away and Father caught sight of a mistily familiar figure open the nearside door after pulling the handbrake so the car would not roll back. The figure, like the others, dissolved in the pearly air. Now the puzzling thing was that the house had a night security guard, a Second World War veteran, his little lodge was built next to the steel gate which was now flung wide open. Although the old soldier used to regale us with stories punctuated with the boom-boom of guns and bazookas in Burma, all he had for a weapon as a guard was a wooden club, a knuckly cudgel, fashioned out of a spiky tree branch distressed with long handling – not with use, certainly the club had been quite idle. It seemed curious that the nightguard stood by while some people were pushing out of the compound the car of one of those who were paying his wages. His quick defence was that he could not say anything because it was Femi, the owner's son, who was in the driver seat, steering the car out of the compound while his friends pushed and one of the friends was Ola, the neighbour's son.

Father was aghast, not to say angry: why would his son orchestrate the—the what, he could not have been stealing the car, could he? No. What was he going to do with it, then? Meanwhile Femi, guessing that Father would certainly have known he was the person in the driver seat, disappeared. He knew he had to do this to avoid rowing with Father. Ola, his friend, feigned ignorance, he said he hadn't seen Femi since the afternoon before, so far as he was concerned the nightguard may have been hallucinating. And where was Femi? Ola could not say.

The next morning Femi left town and went to an aunt's house in Lagos, he said he'd let other people explain to Father why he was trying to freewheel his car out of the compound. Within hours everyone in the house, except Father, got to know what it was all about. The nightguard, who had been trying to protect himself, particularly embarrassed by the bribe of whisky and cigarettes he often took from the boys to open the gate and stand by while the car was being rolled out, explained it all to Father, making no mention of the bribe. Since the start of the summer holidays three weeks before, every weekend Femi and Ola and his other friends had been doing what they were seen doing, they would push the car out of the compound and return it in the early hours of the morning.

What were the boys doing with the car during those hours? Party-crawling, flitting from one house disco and dusky funky discothèque to the other. Femi came of age in the epoch of disco, and sometimes on a Saturday night there might be up to a dozen discos in town, the more ambitious and mobile of the youths might turn up in all of the parties, going from one to the other. Femi had picked up the spare key where it was hung, certain that no one would miss it unless the other went astray. He and his friend Ola then enlisted the help of other stretch-jeansed and T-shirted boys who would all push the car while Femi sat at the driver seat, and out of the compound, as the car gathered momentum on asphalted road, he would start it and speed off.

Although it was still the halcyon days of Nigeria's 'Oil Boom', it was not common for 18-year-olds to have their own cars, and you had to be a son of a millionaire who had many cars before you might be able to drive one to discos. So a boy of 18 'cruising' around in a car, even if it was a banger, would be seen as privileged and he would not just be popular with boys but with girls too. Middle-class families like ours often had one car, usually the preserve of the father, the head of the family, and it would be a most liberal teacher-father who would give the key of such a car to his 18-year-old to party with, and few would grin and shrug it off if they discovered that their son had been night-larking with the car. Femi spent the remainder of the school holiday in Lagos before returning home several weeks later. Father did not say a word about the matter when he saw his son, he actually shrugged.

All of these memories came back to me when I was trying to deal with Femi's death, all of these and more.

His all-too-human struggles. His stay in Europe. His sojourn in England, overlapping that of Marechera's, which might be why they appeared in the same dream (you see, this is what an attempt to be logical about dreams becomes, absurd and far-fetched). Actually, this was the only one I can call a dream, because the night I had the dream was the only night that I slept with any depth for about a couple weeks. Insomnia was part of the grieving *precess*. No, not insomnia, it was depthless sleep, strictured nap, the sort of sleep that would never reach the nirvana, the peace, of deep slumber. It was during this time in the borderland of sleep and wakefulness that I *imagined* I heard my brother narrating the story of the dreadlocked Dada. Or was it me? Or the Dada himself?

Lucid or conscious dreaming? Hypnagogia: the blanket definition of the state between wakefulness and sleep – the hallucinations, the auditory and visual images. Ruminations from the edge of sleep. Threshold thoughts brought on by the lightness of half-sleep, half-wakefulness. Morphean wanderings. And it was simply not a case of falling asleep after a while, my mind was so strung-up that sleep never came and there was no reverting back to full wakefulness, perhaps owing to the horror I have always had of insomnia, of going on for days and nights on end without sleep. I realised even as it happened that this was dream simulation. Why such narratory vision came at the time it came I cannot say, and since it was not really a dream there is no investing it with any Freudian symbolism, no phallicisation of anything, no mucking under the surface to reach for fraternal conflicts. If it was a definitive dream, the Dada tale would mesh better with Jung's theory of archetypes, personal and collective unconscious, but this was a straight, if reverist, retelling of something someone had told me before. I wondered whether it had anything to do with the Dali's picture that the death of my brother had also brought forth. Dali. Dada. Dadaism. And Baba. Because one of Femi's names was Babatunde: *Father has returned to us*. He was born a few days after our grandfather, Father's father, died. During visits to Father's hometown, some of our grandaunts would call him 'Baba'. And in Ifon, mother's hometown, a couple of grandaunts who knew my maternal grandfather well before he died in 1947, twenty years before I was born, also called me 'Baba' because, in their unscientific opinion, I was a small copy of the late ancestor.

And the boy who told me the rather unlikely-seeming story many years before? I didn't see much of Dada after that, but he never left Mother's hometown, never finished primary school. I heard stories of how he had at first become a teenage tearaway, then a taxi station tout, then in his early 20s had trained to become a shaman and while doing this had decided to leave his hair rampant so that he had, now by choice, become a dreadlocked Dada again. The last I heard of him about five years ago was that he had become a powerful voodooman and healer, his locks conferring on him the aura of invincibility, spiritual grandeur and esotericism, plus he made no bones about the fact that cannabis was what he always stuffed in his custom-built pipe and that he was a post-modern medicineman who could listen and dance to Bob Marley and Peter Tosh (a counterpoint of Tosh's *Mystic Man* and *Bush Doctor* was his mantra) and provide spiritual ease to people when they came to him. Before he was 30 he had had three wives in his harem, with a string of girlfriends in tow. Days after I had the Dada dream, I spoke to my mother and I asked about Dada, Mother told me that he passed away three years before.

Supernaturalism is as natural to most African societies as religion itself; it is part of the psychosociology of everyday life. Even evangelical Christianity, which has now become the soul of the continent, is shot through with the bottomless black hole of the paranormal. As a child growing up in Yorubaland, the possibility of an alternative universe was something I took in under the shadow of the overbearing transcendence that religion provided. I, like many, tottered on the edge of the cosmological horizon where reality and irreality exerted their pull from all sides. Spirits were believed to walk with humans, only shaded by their better grasp of the tricks of dimensions-crossing. But beyond invisibility, spirits might decide to take on human form if they so wished, assume the garb of a crone or a belle. I grew up primed with such an unlikely story as that of the fleshed-out wraith of someone who just died elsewhere returning home, to spend hours with his family, even sleep with his wife/widow and then leave the house just as those who had come to announce his passing arrived. There was the post-Freudian tale of the man who shook the hand of someone and found a few moments later that he had been unmanned, that he had suddenly suffered a kind of penile invagination. Pregnant women had to walk with a pebble hidden somewhere in their chemises lest the embryos and foetuses growing in them be displaced by strolling demons. A man took a woman he picked up at the side of the road home and after sleeping with her, the woman shape-shifted into a skeleton – in other words the man had slept with a mischievous self-resurrecting zombie. Most young preteen girls were believed to belong to a kind of pre-Harry Potter world of impish adventures, an alternative world where the she-witchlings seemed to be more at home than the world we knew. A market was often considered a place where every sort of spirit contended for space, for elbow room, for stall-place, especially during noontime, the peak-time of hyperactivity in fairyland – palm-oil bought in a market at this time might as well be blood. Of course age and maturity might mellow how the mind would swallow, process and digest, these overlapping parallel worlds, lush florid clumps of these mythologies remain as part of folk memory, sometimes in a slightly muted, coy way. And today the evangelicals have recalibrated the frontiers of such thoughts by their own ceaseless talk of enemies, battles, demons, witches, principalities and every sort of abstruse oddity or 'entity'.

Dr Tai Solarin, the eminent atheist and humanist, was the most vociferous 'enemy' of supernaturalism in his time, he not only railed against belief in any kind of metaphysical balderdash, he also went out of his way to prove that most of the things that were given importance were foolish superstition and desperate old wives' cow-shit used to daub the edifice of truth and reality in the bid to buff them. He wrote about how he sometimes went out in the early hours of the morning to eat richly-prepared dishes of food placed at crossroads and junctions by those who believed they were trying to appease some sort of god. The point of the food placed in the navel of crossroads was that anyone who ate it – a tramp, say – would have eaten all the ailment of the sick person, that is after the gods had accepted the offering and had perhaps tasted some of it. Now this sounds rubbishy. And, it truly is, because according to Dr Tai Solarin, he polished off a lot of these plates of hoodooed ambrosia, and the great man lived to the ripe old age of 77. There was not even anything like a last geriatric illness for the old humanist, he died the kind of death he wished for himself, a simple straightforward death that would not give 'believers' the pleasure of saying, *'Look at him, he is suffering now because he does not believe in God.'* Dr Solarin tripped while climbing the staircase of his house and a few hours later he exited. Needless to say he was mocked by some religionists: maybe he was going to write an article against God, so God, considering him a pest that could not be suffered again, placed a phantom obstacle in his way or nudged him with his invisible hand.

Dr Solarin's desire that his body be donated to science was not shared by his religion-bound relatives, they told him when he was alive and spry that they would certainly not allow his body to end up on an experimental slab; the relatives also begged him not to leave a testament that his body be burned and the ashes scattered to the four winds. Sheila Solarin, the godless sage's wife, saw to it that he was buried as simply and quickly as he would have liked. Dr Solarin was demonstrably naturalistic to the very last: for him science and reason explained a lot of things, most things, he believed there was absolutely nothing against nature.

Now while I leave my own approach to supernaturalism as open-ended – that is seamlessly sceptical – as my opinion about God, the sort of recall that I had after my brother's death would not be difficult to decipher and interpret, it is no more than what *mere* psychology would explain. For one thing, my mind, my psyche if you like, was in overdrive, thanks to grieving. A million thoughts flicked through my mind at the time, although I may have brought back the Dada story because there was something epic about its scale, its myth-like appearance, its allure, it is the kind of recital – redolent and recognisable – that comes together brilliantly for what philosophers might call 'intentionality,' a term which Wikipedia describes as 'the ability of the mind to form representations.' Even if it was dreamt I do not think it would be beyond the remit of philosophical 'investigators of experience' (phenomenologists) to look into. And it does not matter that by the time my brain was retelling the story, the dreadlocked Dada had also died, which I didn't find too surprising or even significant. We tend to forget that eventually life dies off into death, it is the condition of the human, of the animal, of the animate, of everything, and it does not matter whether a sliver of life is characterised by longevity or brevity, it ends, it peters out. And since dreams are often random and arbitrary, one can just as easily dream of the living as of the dead – it means nothing, it signifies nothing, it bodes nothing, the ghosts of the past comprise the living and dead. If one could have a dream, right out of the blue, of partaking of a spread, I mean table-spread, with the Queen of England or the Obamas, as someone I knew said she did in a dream, there is nothing extraordinary about dreaming of someone one knew, wherever she might be, living or dead.

Truly Femi was not there when Dada told me and Akin the story years before, but does it then mean that they met in a sort of afterworld where Dada told him his story? Unlikely – it was all in my head, this was something that I had stored in a memory card, in my mental wafer, and my grief-surcharged brain had pitched on it and replayed it, regurgitated it. With their notions of Archetypes and Latent/Manifest Meanings, I think both Jung and Freud made too much of dreams, they loaded them with too much significance and mantic hype. Now here is a reason I do believe that dreams, colourful and persuasive as they seem, do not often count for much. It would have been easy and convenient to apply Jungian interpretation, particularly synchronicity, 'meaningful coincidence', to this *faux*-dream but I might as well apply it to every dream I have, which often has as much 'chronicity' as would have spooked me if I did not know it was just part of the habit of my 'sleeping mind'. For instance, I almost always wake up from a dream on the dot of the hour, and usually it is four or five in the morning – right on the dot. Why? I don't know, but that has not made me dissolve into oneiromantic raptures. There may be a number of reasons why this is so. It may be reflexive self-conditioning. It may be the biological clock, the evolution of circadian rhythm reaching a cusp within the limits of those hours. The metronomic regularity of some of my dreams brought itself fully to bear one morning. I am not the deepest of sleepers, I usually wake before six, but I do often use an alarm clock to wake me up at the right time. The night before, I set the alarm clock for six because I wanted to leave home for work at six thirty. But that night I had an unusually extensive beauty sleep, so I would perhaps have needed the alarm if I had not been woken up by the continual jingling of a phantom bell in a rather forgettable dream that I was having. About a couple of minutes to six, something rang clearly, cleanly. I was roused, and I knew straightaway that it was not the clock. I lifted myself from bed and discovered that it was a tick or two from six. Moments later the alarm clock beeped, superfluously. Now imagine I was a born-again Christian and I was to attend a job interview that morning. And to further hypothesise, at the interview I did well, or was seen to have done well, after which I was told to begin work immediately. Imagine the sugary and splendid rendering the negligible and irrelevant dream I had would attract, the rave interpretation, the propitious reconfiguration, hallelujah whoops about how the angels, and not the clock, woke me when it was exactly six o'clock. And it could only be the good angels who made me get the job, who whispered 'take him' in the ear of the interviewer.

Was it more than a coincidence that exactly fifty years to the day Femi was born Akin's daughter, Bose, had a child, a girl: Oct 3 1962/Oct 3 2012? Coincidence or not, the birth day of the beautiful baby will always remind us of Femi, of his own birth day and, inevitably, death day. How different, really, are these two crucial days; what separates them? John Updike wonders succinctly in his poem 'March Birthday, 2002, and After':

'Birthday, death day – what day is not both?'

Passional

I remember now that when I tried to write about the loss of my big sister big brother in an essay, Oscar Wilde's wicked wisdom had strained to suggest itself: *To lose one parent may be regarded as a misfortune, to lose both looks like carelessness.* Would it ever be acceptable to say: *To lose one sibling may be regarded as a misfortune, to lose two looks like carelessness*? Well, for me I don't think it would ever be funny unless I put it in the mouth of a character in a Wilde-parodying piece of dark humour, although if I did that I might end up parodying myself instead of Oscar Wilde. And there is something about the loss of one's brother or sister, older or younger, early in life, which makes impossible to be flippant about it. Now if I didn't know my parents very well and had lost them when they were younger, I suspect I would, nonetheless, have been able to use this Wildean wit to qualify their passing. There is something distant about one's parents' seniority, a remove, a chasm, that is temporally straddled by one's siblings, however early or late the sibling came. Besides, there is a sense of mutual complementariness between siblings that even if you were mortal enemies you would know a bit of you had disappeared when they predeceased you. In spite of myself, I sometimes found myself alluding to the loss of my brother and sister, especially when stressing to someone that this had little or nothing to do with what I believed and did not believe, although I never neglected to say that the bereavements were, anyhow, enough reason to be indifferent to the idea of a loving, magnanimous, do-gooder God. And to stretch the loop, I did tend to say that in the larger global scheme of things, the loss was minor, minor in an objective impersonal sense, but crucial to me. Along the lines of this thinking, when I wrote about the Haitian earthquake in which thousands of people perished, a quip which was almost Wildean in its delivery had found its way into the article. To give it context, I will take two paragraphs from the piece:

> *In the years between 1986 and 2001, I lost a sister and brother. The fact that I still have four siblings has not made it easier that I lost two. Of course, my apprehension of mortality in a secular way may actually have made it possible for me to take it better than someone who goes to church and believes a superavuncular God owes him and his kin the boon of longevity. I tend not to blame any sort of god for the bereavements, not even during the first one when I – an adolescent – was limbering up for the leap unto scepticism. But then again, how does one begin to excuse the dearth of God's magnanimity in the deaths of a young woman of 28 and a young man of 39 in what may be described as the 'prime' of their lives..? Few theologians would be able to explain the point of a ten-year-old, for instance, laid low by cancer for years, wracked with pain and grave discomfiture, before he finally succumbed. The child's parents would rather they have him in this world than in any sort of fuzzy afterlife where their chances of seeing or sharing any future space with him are as dim and as narrow as the inside of a coffin, although recently, a Scottish Christian*

> *fundamentalist came to an agreement with his wife that he should follow their son who died in a road accident to heaven so that the poor boy would not be lonely there.*
>
> *I do not know why I always take the pains to tell people that I have not shunned religion because of the loss of my siblings. But I, consciously, have not. In spite of what such a coalescent loss might do to the psyche I would not like it to be the case that nonbelief in any sort of imaginary 'heavenly father' is predicated on personal loss. Any more than I would think it sensible to throw tantrums in the direction of the Devil after the minutest misstep. It is not unique that I lost a brother and a sister, there are worse things in this Bible-christened vale of tears, a vale variously booby-trapped, if you allow, by* God. *The picture of human misery is larger and bulkier than what a mere family album with its inscribed RIPs can carry.*

The penultimate sentence was where a bit of Voltairean – not Wildean – wit had insinuated itself into an otherwise sober, if straight-spoken, essay. (Wilde was an irreverent irrelevance who sought to profane and ruffle a poker-faced essay.) Again, I quoted the above paragraphs to show how close the writing of it was to when my younger sister, Adejoke, aged 38 years, died of cancer of the liver – only a few months. Now if I were the one who fell sick and died, I am sure some extreme Christians – in the way one talks of an extreme drug-juiced sportsman, for instance – might, in the spirit of *schadenfreude*, which is not entirely alien to their religion, say that it was what I had been writing about God and the Christian religion which caused such a thing to happen (I will come to that later). But Adejoke, besides being naturally pleasant and good-natured, was a Christian. About a year before she died I visited Nigeria with my family and the degree to which she had taken her Christianity was as high as could possibly be in the alarmingly religion-stricken Nigeria.

I looked forward to seeing Adejoke. I had not been in Nigeria for years and she had come to the Lagos International Airport to pick me and my family up. We embraced warmly. I was happy to see she was looking good, she was the picture of health. Inside her car I opened the glove compartment to stow the book I was reading on the plane away, but there was a book in the compartment. *A* bible, I noticed immediately, and there was a small silver cross.

I said, 'You keep these things in your car?'

She said, 'What things?'

'A bible and a cross—'

She said, 'Yes, I keep them there. Oh, I remember—you said the Bible is just a book.'

'And, my dear sister, I am sorry it is still only a book. And the cross is only an object that may not really have had anything to do with Jesus.'

A woman of few words, Adejoke only smiled and said nothing. I suspect that what I had become before I left Nigeria had returned to her: the godless stray sheep of the family (It would be an awful pun to say the 'stray *black* sheep of the family,' wouldn't it?). I decided to leave my book on my lap as she drove us home. I even reprimanded myself momentarily, I hadn't seen my sister in years and I thought I had said too much even in the few words that I uttered. I should just shut up and leave her to practise her Christianity the way she wanted. We grew up in a house where there was a certain freedom to take religion as lightly or as keenly as one pleased, although my trenchant objections to religion and doubts about what the word 'God' really meant might not have been expected, it was never something anyone lost sleep over. It was during this visit to Nigeria that I realised how completely out of kilter my faithlessness in any sort of god was in the veritable God's Acre that Nigeria had become. Indigestibly monstrous and jarring was my churchlessness, my difficult-to-hide allergy to the mush of piety in which everyone seemed to have steeped themselves, overgorging themselves. Someone who came to visit Adejoke the day – Sunday – after we arrived in her house asked whether I would be going to church. My sister, solicitous as ever, said we came in late the night before and were too tired to go to church. Well, we came in pretty late the night before, but whether the tiredness brought on by turning in late had taken the thought of church-going from my mind or the fact that I would not have attended anyway, was a different matter. But my sister was well-intentioned, she at least moved the burden of answering from me, and she must have suspected how candid, even cavalier, the answer I would give would be: *I don't do church*, say. I do not know how well I would have couched the answer, but there is no doubt that I would have declared that I do not normally attend church on Sundays. And inevitably I would have come across like any feisty atheist in Britain would appear to a Christian or a Muslim when holding forth: arrogant, sniffy, dismissive and clever-clever – well, that is how unfeisty atheists seem to appear to the religious, anyway. It is often hard to be seen as the soul of humility, or even sanity, while sitting in a room where everyone but you believes in the realness of the Tooth Fairy, it does not help to say that you would need to see the Tooth Fairy, or would like to ascertain she turned up physically to remove a tooth from under your four-year old daughter's pillow: why not simply put yourself in the head of your daughter and suspend disbelief like everyone appears to have done? Something I have learnt over the years is that I should not even try to be mealy-mouthed about what I think of God or religion, because any effort I make only defeats its end, and I always end up voicing out my opinions, anyway. If anyone asked why I didn't go to church and I began with 'I am tired' or something, I might ask a moment later, 'By the way, why must I go to church?'

Even if the fancy ever flickered through my mind that I should attend church when I went to Nigeria, I would have liked to go to a certain church. Now there was the Anglican church of my childhood, St Andrew's Cathedral, newly finished when I started primary school in the same compound more than 30 years before. The church was indeed worth revisiting. It was a grand house of Christian worship and I am sure it would still remain a fine place, marmoreal externals and all that, and I might not even feel that sense of dissolution and abandonment that Larkin feels about the church he visits in *Church Going*. I understand that with the intention of tuning in to the prevailing spirit of Pentecostalism in Nigeria, Anglican parishes and churches have jazzed up their act, they have downplayed solemnity and their slow-motion style of worship, they have moved towards evangelicalism, towards ambidoxy.

The New Church. This was the church I thought of attending – not any Sunday service, or any mass – there was something about the unfinishedness of the church, its peripherality, which drew me. What has become of the New Church? How many people now attend the church? How many Swedenborgians remain in the town? Has the New Church also pepped up, renewed itself, tarted itself up, now that the whole of the country has almost become the stamping ground of giddy

Pentecostals? And I wished to see the bas-reliefs of Swedenborg again, do a multiple-take – for who knows what this prophet who predicted the hyper-Christian future of Africa would be *feeling* now? Oh yes, he might still be feeling things, seeing things. For an uber-religious man who believed strongly in heaven and hell, especially heaven, he might be up there in the empyrean smilingly gratified with the many millions of worship houses that have sprung up in Africa, a fulsome fulfilment of his vision. His carven image might wink at me. He might even talk to me, chasten me for being an undiscipular 'disbeliever,' a sceptic.

I didn't have the time to visit the New Church before I returned to the UK. Again now, with retrospective wistfulness, I remember the flight back to England. I left my family in Lagos, they still had two weeks to spare before they would return. I sat beside a young couple who talked a lot about their future (I couldn't help but eavesdrop). The couple had closed their eyes and their lips had moved in prayer when the plane began to soar, and six hours later when it began to descend. Besides inevitably and extraneously overhearing some of the chats of the prayerful pair, I spent most of the time reading Irvin Yalom's *Schopenhauer's Cure*, a novel that I bought because of the name of Schopenhauer rather than that of the author, who was not known to me until I was looking for something on Schopenhauer and found him. *Schopenhauer's Cure* is a good if anodyne novel which approaches the great philosopher's ideas and life in a balanced and unpedantic manner.

Schopenhauer's *The World as Will and Representation* was perhaps the first philosophical work which made me think that philosophy might be more interesting than it was being given credit for. I later read the pungent vignette that is *On the Suffering of the World* and it seemed to have woken me up from a dreamful slumber in which I looked at the world with rose-coloured goggles. And what has been described as *Suffering of the World*'s 'pessimism' had appeared to me like the most unvarnished, if steely, exploration of Truth that I had ever read: in spite of our best efforts, the life of every existent – human and animal – is difficult, desperate and sad, and although there are ways to relieve the drudge and ache of existence, God and the so-called revealed religions have nothing to do with it. Schopenhauer's philosophy may not offer any sunny consolations (it offers mild leaven), but it does certainly provoke serious thoughts about the lineaments of the dead horse that is the meaning of life. Schopenhauer's philosophy may not provide us with any whip to join in the orgy of carcass-flogging, but it tells us to look closely at the bathos of the beating the late horse is still taking. Schopenhauer's cosmos is not easy to contemplate, let alone inhabit, which is why a noun like 'Schopenhauerian' has never been popular, because the philosopher has become so identified with unrelieved pessimism that he now comes at the top of a vinegary food-chain of misanthropes.

Also integral to Schopenhauer's worldview is antinatalism, the school of 'better never to have been born'. In *On the Suffering of the World*, he writes that whenever he sees a child, his thoughts, as would have been natural for a dyed-in-the-wool 'crapehanger', do not err towards when the child will die anytime in the nearest or farthest future, but when she will begin to live, when she will become nature's punchbag, pummelled, coshed, bashed, mauled – and, of course, finally crushed to a pulp. Schopenhauer believes that humans live in a permanent state of pain, discomfiture and hurt, to use an antinatalist term, and he tries to offer ways by which humans can relieve the painful stomachache and the corresponding shittiness of life – by music, for instance.

While I would not describe myself as an out-and-out miserabilist, even before I knew there was anyone called Schopenhauer I had my opinions about the purpose and point of human existence, the inkling that it is massively exaggerated and embroidered with meaning and gilt had begun to crystallise. One of the first teachings of Christianity that I doubted and completely rejected, even when I was still attending church, was the bugbear of heaven and hell. By the time I was ten it had begun to sound preposterous to me, and this was not helped by the film of Lazarus and Dives I saw a couple of years before. I came to believe that even if God was going to judge anyone on any Last Day, he would have to invent somewhere more plausible to send the judged, not any vast spumous lake of quenchless fire or any lush garden of deathless bliss. By the time I lost my incrementally dulled appetite for religion I had come to see that for the majority of people life was hellish, anyway. I looked and couldn't find anyone for whom life was seamlessly heavenly – mundanely and momentarily happy maybe, but it would take a kind of yet-undiscovered Huxleyan dope to induce unblinking bliss.

To the extent that I agree with philosopher Colin Radford, as he writes in his book *Driving to California*, that we live philosophy everyday of our lives, I remember giving a rather startling, somewhat Schopenhauerian, answer to a question my brother, Akin, asked one afternoon when I was about 20. Together with some other members of the family, we were discussing the past and Akin had said the name of a boy we used to play with; he had wondered what would have become of the boy after more than a decade since he left the neighbourhood, when his parents moved out of the neighbourhood. I replied, 'He would only be somewhere if he was alive, he might be dead.'

I remember Mother admonishing me, 'Why would you say such a thing? He might be in university. He would be about your age.' Akin's seemingly innocuous question was a Pandora's Box of sorts, philosophically it could even spawn a tome of both hopeful and hopeless probabilities. The fact that the person in question was of a similar age as me should not give anyone any assurance that he would still be living, even Mother would know this, Christian optimist though she was, she only did not want me to overspeculate on where the boy was or what he might be doing, and even if I tried to surmise anything at all it should be something cheery. Even if the boy we used to know turned out to be still alive and kicking, the counterfactual that I came up with was still relevant to the matter at hand, which fundamentally, was that the very accident of living, and its often concealed pitfalls and obstacles, always ends one way and one way only.

If the answer I gave about the whereabouts of the boy seemed like Schopenhauerian overkill, I had not forgotten there might be other possibilities too. He might truly be studying one good course or the other in a university. But he might also be puffing too much marijuana smoke, losing himself in it, anteing up the odds of schizotypy. He might yet become a prodigy of commerce, make good but yet set himself up for a prodigal dissipation. He may have become a born-again Christian (more likely), singing hosannas and speaking in tongues in a church. There indeed was a world of tarot possibilities, positive shuffled with negative, which could suggest itself in the circumstances. And I hoped that I was able to persuade everyone that considering the probability of the subject's mortality had less to do with morbidity than with juggling the many skittish sticks of casualism (chance and accident), any of which stick could take on a life of its own and fly off at a tangent, of the fickleness of the good old Lady Fortune, how she could morph into anything at any time she pleased.

Akin and I often had mutual friends, even before we were out of teenagehood a couple of friends had been taken away through car crashes, and yet another who died just some months before may have wrung out the answer I gave. Ojo, a tall, well-built young man, part-timing his way through university while working as a teacher, was burdened by family exigencies, having to financially care for two younger siblings and a sick mother – and he was only 22. He was a passenger in an intercity minibus taxi, and somewhere along the way, the driver, possibly high on something, summarily finished off the lives of every passenger in the ten-seater vehicle, including that of himself. This sort of 'accident' is not uncommon in Nigeria. Personally, I know up to a dozen people who have lost their lives in crashes, and the ironic thing is that before the start of every trip between towns or cities in any sort of commercial vehicle, from cars to coaches, someone always took it upon herself to invite others to join her in praying. Since the passengers have only just been thrown against one another, the thrust of the prayer is the adjuration of safety for the duration of the journey. It is always an elaborate devotional ritual in which every voice in a coach or bus will pipe up, passionately calling forth a dash of the Blood of Jesus on the coach and on everyone in it, appealing to God to be the real driver of the coach, to take the steering wheel away from the person in the driving seat, take control of the coach himself and personally deliver them to where they are going. I do not know why people forget that this sort of interactive, ambulatory God that breathes, speaks, shits and does every sort of thing humans do, had withdrawn himself since he rumbled Adam and Eve and cursed them in a fit of wrathful umbrage. Okay, maybe they only want God to take over the coach *in spirit*, after all, everyone knows Jesus is not likely to arrive and throw bucketloads of his blood on the coach. I can't imagine anyone who had seen the carnage on Nigerian roads bringing up any image of blood, even if it was that of Jesus – but people do, daily.

There is no doubt that few of those praying for divine protection would also have considered a mixed-bag of reasons crashes might happen. The matter of road safety. The witches and evildoers amongst them whose countervailing power would challenge the apotropaic (ability to ward off evil) power of God. The probability of the driver's carelessness. The sins of any or all of the passengers which may call down the wrath of God, something which may lead to associative justice and other freewillist arguments that a clever theologian would use to explain away any occurrence of a bad crash. And there may be the argument from negative theology that God cannot have been responsible as he is incapable of doing anything bad or evil, God is always fair, good and right-minded (if he had anything like a mind), an argument which will ultimately remove God from the picture so much so that the pointlessness of praying to him in the circumstances should intrude upon the mind of the thoughtful, although it seems as if it never does.

One such terrible 'accident' had also given me further insight into how religion, especially the Semitic ones, may confer on its practitioner a certain particularist entitlement, a sense of electhood. A 70-year-old friend of Mother's travelled to the state capital to see her son, she was one of ten passengers in a minibus whose driver may have been far-gone on anything from drink to cannabis. Some ten miles into the journey, the squiffy shithead crashed the bus and killed nine of his passengers, only he and the 70-year-old woman survived. Just like the driver, the septuagenarian friend of my mum came away with minor injuries, she only spent a few hours in the hospital before she was released. Among those who otherwise died were two teenagers, three young men in their early 20s, fresh from university, travelling to where they would do their national service, a mother and her baby. Like most of the crashes on Nigerian roads this was a sad and avoidable waste of lives, but Christian that she was the septuagenarian thought it would not be a bad thing to attend church a couple of Sundays later, and not just to worship but to celebrate and give thanks to God for preserving her life while others died, and as is often the case, her pastor would play the vicarial conduit through which the gratitude would reach her good God. After church there would be a reception in the house of the elderly woman. I appealed to Mother to attend neither the thanksgiving nor the reception. In spite of the efforts of the best and most brilliant of apologetics, it is a fact that Christianity and logic do not mix so much, but I think that in spite of antinomian argument for faith, blind, unquestioning faith, there is a relationship of sorts between morality and Christianity.

Unprepossessing as what the good elderly woman who survived the crash did appear to be, her behaviour easily bore out Schopenhauer's argument that although ultimately every human life is marked by misfortune, we all tend to measure our luck or lack of it against that of others. So beyond Christianity, the celebration of the old woman's life in a church was somewhat natural. Wasn't there, indeed, something lucky about a woman who has reached the age the good God of the Bible says is enough for anyone before she clocks out surviving a crash in which an 18-month-old infant died? What, to be sure, does this say about a loving, fair God, whose ears, as Christian theology would have it, are not exactly deaf to the sort of *Te Deum* the woman sang to him, who even commands this as integral to Judeo-Christian creed?

The infant who died in the accident was not unique, thousands of innocents are despatched in painful, even gruesome, ways every day and as I have written somewhere else, these children may not even have the benefit of limbo again, because the Catholic Church appears to be slowly waking up to the absurdity of that superfluous midway house to heaven. Again, what, who, killed the child in the crash, who and what kills the thousands of helpless infants who perish every day? God? Certainly not. Maybe the can-carrying poor Devil. Or Herod. Or Moloch. Or an ogre, a creature much-feared by children. And if such not entirely luckless children were born to a Yoruba parent, he might have been named the celebratory Ayomide just months or even days before – Ayomide, *My joy has arrived* – besides other sweetly propitious names like Oluwaseun, *I am grateful to God*. So if such a child died who, pray, was the killjoy who took the parents' happiness away? Anyhow, ultimately, the parents had to turn to God for consolation after a tremulous and snivelling rage against him. (And the children who are 'taken away' are not exactly luckless because, at least, they have escaped the drudge of adulthood, the difficulties of old age).

Now however reasonable I think antinatalism is I can never be its practiser again. I have children of my own, and as it happens, one even has the middle name of Ayomide – *Joy*, in a word, a name given her by one of her grandmothers, (and so far, my girl has given everyone tremendous joy, joy mixed with the natural niggling rogueries of children). But you see, my children are not my clones, they have a mother who has her own views. So if, for my part, I could take the thoughtless risk of bringing them into the world, I could just as well go ahead, with a fortuitous sense of duty and with the nod of their mother, and give them names that I knew might or might not have any direct bearing on how things turn out. I would not call a child that I chose to have *My joy has not come*, that would be taking antinatalism to pathological extremes, that would be what has been described as *misopaedia*: hatred of children, particularly one's own children.

An essay I wrote and published on the eve of the millennium was entitled 'Happy New Year'. It was an exercise in philosophical irony, an unseasonable carefree caveat which proclaims that as we light our bonfires, fire our crackers and sing the carols, we must also remember that fires die out sometimes too quickly, crackers fail to crack, and that we may sing the carols today but chant a dirge tomorrow and even altogether lose our voice the day after. While strongly agreeing that we humans cannot live without rituals and habit, I pointed out that having 'naming ceremonies' and birthday parties may not be as important as many think they are. In the first part of another essay called *What's in a Name*, I tried to deconstruct – self-destruct would be the better word – the sense of my name, both first and last, having given up the middle one for some years. I gave an explanation of Oriku, how it is not a common Yoruba surname, its boundary-busting exoticness, cosmopolitanism, its Japanese flavour, its higher occurrence in Kenya. I wrote about how Adebowale had meant something at the time I was given the name and how it had turned out to be meaningless and vain because within a few months it became clear that it meant nothing.

There is something called 'royal families' in Yoruba towns, families from which kings or chiefs, or whatever you want to call them in English, were chosen. A town may have several branches of a royal family, not-too-distantly related members of 'houses', whose kinship has been fractured by contentious contests for the throne of the town. I came from one of the branches of such a 'royal family' in Father's hometown. An uncle and someone from another arm of the royal family had been tussling over the throne, taking the fight even as far as the courts, long before I was conceived. Just before I arrived there was the certainty that my uncle was going to become 'king' of the town, everyone had hoped that a few days after I was born there would be a fulfilment of the Shakespearean promise. I was given the name Adebowale, that is *The crown has come to our house*, in anticipation of the arrival of the crown on my uncle's doorsteps a few days later. Well, even as I write 40-odd years later, the crown has not arrived – and the uncle, heir putative, died long ago, uncrowned. The other man became king after a court injunction stopped my uncle from staking a claim to the throne. For me, my name has always been a byword for why it is hollow wishful thinking to pay heed to the meaning of any name one gives a child, just as a child who died too soon should be a kind of *danse-macabre* reminder that naming ceremonies, while it is all right to have one, should not be turned into a fanfare.

Now I can be self-deprecating, ironic, humorous, satiric and even caustic just about anything, not least in some of the literary work I produce. One of the poems that anyone who has read some of my light verse would believe without benefit of elucidation was written in a moment of creative frivolity and playfulness, is *On the*

Evening of the Nativity of Younger Sister. And it would seem all the more droll if the reader knew it was written just after I had concluded that even if there was anything like Jesus' nativity, there was – allowing for the margin of miraculous chance – nothing like Immaculate Conception, and that the birth itself might not be as momentous as the gospels have made it. Cold, detached, metascriptural analysis aside, the Nativity story, as cherry-picked in the gospels, is still one of the most enchanting tales ever written. Taken collectively, it is beautiful, self-contained, charming and stirring, it made so much impression on me as it has made on billions of people. Even though now I know that dozens of Eastern gods and avatars were mythically conceived in the same way as Jesus, I think the Nativity story is marvellous, marvellously told. In the grip of poetic inspiration, I decided to write about the birth of my younger sister, Adejoke, when she was 17 and I was 21, and the only fitting backdrop that I could give the truly happy event was the Nativity narrative:

'I'll take you to go see your newborn sister,'
Dad says to us all, cradling me in his arm,
smallest of the children, long-styled Baby of the
Family. And to me: 'You've got a little sister now.
You will grow to love her, won't you?'
But I've suddenly grown older as the taunts of all
tell me, from the tyrant throne of Family's Baby
I've been thrown, overthrown, and in a momentary
pique of ego I thought she must be an afterthought.
And sister, a baby sister, why not brother, baby
brother like I am to another with whom I kick
and run? Oh, isn't a baby sister better than a boy,
gentler, kinder, will she be able to outrun me to the
family love-seat?

Well, we'll see.
Dad's dusk drive through the gates is to me
a drive through a deathless diseaseless place,
a paradise of groomed grass and topiarised trees.
St Louis Hospital welcomes us to the catholicity
of healingdom and the nun-nurses I see
I can only call angels and saints, crisp-habited, trim,
maidenly, gloriously calico-capped
like the genius of life and love. A marmoreal
Madonna rises between a rosebush
and an hibiscus hedge,
crooking a free finger at us – and she we follow
into Maternity Ward whose blue-gloss walls are
silvered with fluorescent lighting. What a
charming place this is: white-linened beds and their
footnoting copies in which I like and love
to snuggle, but they do seem too little, too cramped
for me. In the cradles I glimpse little doll-size
things. Little babies, I know, newborns.
Just as the rhyme 'My Mother' rises unbidden,
I suddenly see mothers, lying, sitting abed,
suckling, all serene-faced, bliss-visaged, bright-
faced for these babies who will be kings, queens and
Croesuses tomorrow. Or what else would be wished
these cherubic beings?

And Mummy, Mother, my mother, our mother,
in her corner bed cradling the new she-tyrant,
sleepingly frowning even now, the newly-arrived tiny
vixen who will unseat me.
I take my eyes away, up, and I catch on a cottered
corner shelf a china Virgin Mother, cradling baby
Jesus, and there is watchful Joseph, all glorious,
gloriole-crowned. In the manger I see
the sheep too, and the Three Wise Men
giving their gifts. I am held long, enraptured,

for there also is a lone star the Wise Men had followed...
And, hey, this star is real, shining through the glazed east window, backgrounding the tableau of Jesus' Nativity. Could this then be the self-same star the Wise Men saw?

Oh, I'll see...
And what I see is Mother and Babe, the suckling, transfigured, haloed, Father
a beaming proud Joseph and three big brothers
three wise men bearing the gifts,
gifts of love, love and love again. And what can I be now but a little lamb, big sisters ewes, all savouring the warmth of this quaint birthplace this early September evening.
Meek Christian lamb that I am all I can offer
my newborn sister is again love, and with sheep's
eye that I see my big sisters make at their newborn
copy what they give I have no doubt about:
Love and love again...in this cool silent
September night when my baby sister is born.

Even as I repeated the poem I knew I was cloying it up a bit, but then I could not help it. Although the needle would only flicker on the memory scale, I can bring back, in an inchoate kind of way, some of my experiences from the age of three, before the arrival of Adejoke, how I used to run after Akin, worry him, tug at his clothes, pinch his hand. I remember how I used to stand at the foot of the old-style couch in our living room and call out to Akin, who was standing some distance away, to come and lie on the seat, and child that he also was, he always thought I was truly unselfish enough to allow him to lie on the couch which was often the preserve of the youngest child in the house, he would start to move and I would fling myself on the slim elegant seat. I was still playing this game when Adejoke arrived. And from the moment Father announced that we should go and see her in the hospital, I immediately became enamoured with the idea of having a younger sibling. Peering over her cot to spy her tiny swaddled frame was also a refreshing soul-distilling experience. I felt good, which is why I think the maternity ward visit stands out clearer than anything that happened to me at the time, and the picture was no less vivid when I wrote the lines some twenty years later.

Layering the poem with a surfeit of love was also a genuine gesture. Seeing my baby sister in her cot was indeed love at first sight, pure, simple, uncomplicated love and I believe this was what her other six siblings felt. Eight days later she was named Adejoke, *She who must be mollycoddled by all*. My sister's name, in contrast to mine, became her, it betokened the love and affection we would all lavish on her all of her life. As parodic and gooey as the poem might seem to some of its readers, it was written with honesty and seriousness of intention. She was the baby of the family, she was our baby; it was a privilege we were all happy to confer – even me who was the baby not long before! Even with the arrival of Adejoke, our parents had experienced rebirth, or rechristening of a sort.

Up till I was seven I was calling Father 'Baba', a tag that I found my older siblings using and had naturally picked up. At the time I was born and was growing this was not unusual, bucolic and earthy as it might sound, especially in a family which had the privilege of middle-class education. The role and status of the father was unchallengeably superior and lofty that nothing but Baba would be correct and proper. Mothers were called

'Mama'. Mama in the family was just as important, although less imposing than Baba, she represented the entire body on which the Pauline head of the father, the Baba, was perched. Mama kept things together in the house; she was, not to put too fine a point on it, the domestic motherboard. Mother was the Mama of the house in every way, but while I found myself using Baba for my father, I called Mother 'Aunty', which was what those who came before me called her. People were often surprised that we addressed our mother as Aunty, to many this was singular and quizzically unreasonable, if not slightly impertinent, because in the English-born vernacular, even today Aunty is an honorific that is interchangeable with Sister. For a lot of people it was improper to address one's mother as Aunty, more so by a younger child like me.

Calling Mother Aunty had come to me by simple suggestibility. It began with the first child, Dupe, who found that two young relatives living with his parents when he began to babble addressed Father as 'Brother' and Mother as 'Aunty', so he called Mother 'Anti' and, curiously enough, instead of calling Father Brother, the idioglossia that came out sounded something like Baba and with the encouragement of everyone around Baba had stuck over against Aunty. For more than 20 years it was Baba and Aunty. I remember one of my playmates wondering why I had called my mother Aunty, was I crazy or something, where was my sense of filial correctness?

It was Adejoke who first addressed Mother as 'Mummy' and who replaced Baba with 'Daddy'. She started with calling them Baba and Aunty until she was about four, and gradually the process of pre-emption began, almost unnoticeably. Soon everyone realised what was going on, a nomenclatural revolution was afoot in the house and the spirit behind it was the youngest in the family, Adejoke. I do not know how Father felt about Baba being replaced by the smart and cool 'Daddy'. Although Mother was amazed at her own renaming, she understood that Adejoke may have picked up Mummy from the television, for instance, a contraption which entered the family home for the first time a couple of years after she was born. Or it could have been a function of the necessary embourgeoisement of the educated classes which came with Nigeria's new-money status brought on by petrodollars, but she found the quiet insistence of her youngest child on calling her Mummy and her father Daddy unobjectionably proper. It was all the more interesting because, barely a year after Adejoke revised how she addressed her parents, all of her older siblings, from me upwards, were also saying Mummy and Daddy, effectively emulating Adejoke – and the handles had stuck. In as far as there is not often an age-appropriate upgrade from Mummy and Daddy to Mum and Dad in Nigerian-English register, even now I as well as my big sister and brothers still call Mother Mummy. Although this seeming infant-speak might be blamed on the demands of linguistic localism, the very act of uttering 'Mummy' was a monument to love, not just love of the mother herself, not even love for Adejoke, but for simple loveliness of the charming and thing she had done: the pithy Platonic resource, the gut yet dutiful decision to call Mother Mummy instead of Aunty and then transmitting this to everyone in the family, passing it round like a cocktail of selfless philtre in a loving-cup.

I might very well have become a well-rounded antinatalist if I had not peered over the cot at my sister that September morning in 1971. It lingers fragrantly even now, fondly, piningly, what I sighted in the cot. I remember her birthdays too, particularly her first, second and third, the third was a feast. And her tenth, she was now feted by her two big sisters, who spared no expense and invited their own friends to celebrate their kid sister's birthday. It was 1981, a year of several rites of passage in the family. Besides Adejoke's birthday, Grandma passed away and Big Sister gave birth to Yejide on the same day. During primary school, Adejoke followed Father for four years to Government Primary School where he was headmaster and followed Mother to St Moses for the remaining two years. She attended a Catholic secondary school, St Louis, a girls-only school, adjoined to the hospital in which she – and I – was born. The age gap between me and Adejoke was such that I was in the final year in secondary school when she began. Fleetingly, I had wished that she started in the coeducational that I was attending. But then within a few months of her years in the girls' school, she began to play Cupid, or Cupid's arrow, or more appropriately, the bearer of love letters, between me and my, *faute de mieux*, first girlfriend.

There is no point harping on Adejoke's personality. I think few people would find it in their hearts to criticise the passion with which I write about my sister, because to some extent I believe in the Socratic posit of the innate goodness of human nature so much so that even if I gushed how unassailably lovely my sister was, very few would or should sniff at it. Maybe I am just being Panglossian, but then since it was not likely that I would traduce her even if she was a fiery gorgon, I still have some reservation about overemphasising her qualities. But this much I would say: Adejoke returned the tideless flow of affection and caring from her brothers and sisters, to the very end she was a dependable sister, ready to help if it was within her moral and material means. All right, Adejoke and I did spar once, we sparred with each other while wearing kid gloves, or was it just a light pillow fight because I don't really know what word would describe the inconsequentialness of the exchange? Possibly just about the time I was writing the ode to her siblinghood we had had the good-natured, and implicitly Freudian, argument about who Mother liked most. Adejoke began the tiff. After having enjoyed an innings of parental as well as brotherly and sisterly pampering to her heart's content, she came home from school one day while I was sitting with Mother in the porch of our house and mustered the cheek to declare, 'Mummy, do you realise Ade is your favourite.'

This was not a comment Mother, or any mother, wanted to hear, not from anyone, certainly not from any of her children, still less from her youngest offspring. Mother and I protested even as I noticed Adejoke's arch smile. I was able to rationalise simply, 'Here is a 17-year-old girl experiencing teenage angst.' But then 'angst' was a word that only made lexical sense to me, and as far as Adejoke was concerned it was a misusage – this was a young woman who had sailed through adolescence like a dream, a pleasant dream. Adejoke embodied the balmy balance, the extended period of eutaxy (opposite of entropy) most families experience before something happens, a tragedy for instance, that might unfix everyone from their alcoves of complacency. I knew the comment she made must have been thrown away, tongue-in-cheek. Or was it? As Mother had mildly protested, she is beyond parental favouritism. From all appearances, her capacity to respond to all of her children's well-being is amazing, or shall we say, natural? But looking back now, for the three of us who came after one another, bringing up the rear, I, in spite of being a boy, seemed to have more to talk to Mother about, and mostly I shared some of the things that I had read in books with her. She had read Chinua Achebe's *Things Fall Apart*, but when I reread *Arrow of God*, I didn't stop pestering her until she read it, and then Wole Soyinka's *Ake*. I remember she found Soyinka risibly lippy for calling his mother 'Wild Christian'. I being the storyteller of the family, Mother was always a patient loyal audience, second only to Akin. So in a way Adejoke had a point, even if she had not taken herself seriously saying what she said. And if Sigmund Freud were listening in, he might strongly and determinedly support my sister. The great man would overstretch my sister's declaration into a warped tightrope of neurosis and then try to navigate it with great skill. But I would seek to unbalance Freud, argue with him, that he tended to read too much into the relationship between mothers and sons, and that although Father had died at the time, I did not kill him, nor did I ever wish him dead and that I missed him badly – in a word, I did not suffer from Oedipal complex as Freud would have liked to make himself believe. And to call what Adejoke said a mere joke is to fall into another Freudian trap, because just as in dreams, a joke in the Freudian context may signify an expression of what has been suppressed, a scented fart released straight from the dark entrails of the unconscious. So one might as well say Adejoke meant what she said, but without malice, without any sour self-satisfaction, without bile, because everything had concluded in a banter, with a cousin who had come in with Adejoke giving her own opinion about why she thought I might be Mother's favourite: I looked like her most, we shared the same frontal gap in our teeth, I smiled like her – these and other trifling divagations which I naturally considered idle flummery.

Adejoke studied to be a secretary and an administrator for four years in the polytechnic. When she was in the first year, the evangelical girlfriend I had at the time was in the final year in the polytechnic and again, Adejoke had played a role in conveying written and verbal messages between us. The girlfriend discussed my budding irreligiousness with my sister, my pigheaded 'freethinker' sensibility, how concerned she was that she might one day lose me if I did not become born-again. Adejoke said she told her maybe one day God would bring me back to the fold, but she quickly explained to me that she had to tell her that to make her relax. Years later, when the girl wrote to me to inform me she'd moved on, seeing that I might never be born-again, I gave the letter to Adejoke to read and after perusing it with a darkening demeanour, she lifted her head, stared at me, and said, 'You lost such a good person because you would not be religious.' I shrugged and said, 'Look, Adejoke, that is how it is with life, win some, lose some, and sometimes we lose good things, things that are dear to us – persons that are dear to us.'

After finishing her national service, Adejoke got married. She was 24 and the wedding was an occasion of colour and circumstance, and of reunion. She lived with her family in the 'oil city' of Port Harcourt, and before I travelled out of the country in 1998 I went to see a friend in the city and stopped for a couple of nights at Adejoke's who was pregnant with her third child, her only daughter, Simi. That would have been the last time I would see my sister if I did not travel to Nigeria in July 2009. Adejoke had made the visit to Nigeria worth the while for me and my family. She took a week off work and chose to take us in her car to wherever we were going in the dreadful Lagos traffic, although she was continually thwarted by the lousy traffic so much that she had to retain a chauffeur who drove us around sometimes. My wife and children had spent another two weeks with her after I returned to the UK.

It was almost exactly a year after the visit to Nigeria that Adejoke died. And the weeks before it happened were some of the most desperate of my life – quiet, stoic, simmering desperation. From the likelihood that she was suffering from mere typhoid, a not uncommon disease in Nigeria, to near-certain diagnosis of cancer, and the face-shutting fateful update of metastasis. How can one sleep or even sit patiently when one knows that one's younger sister is slipping away. The beautiful baby one once knew. The toddler who would not tarry on a spot on her second birthday for the photographer to get a good snap. The little girl who used to cry when her mother was plaiting her hair and had to be offered sweets as a sop. The girl who would come back from school running around in her brown-gymslip uniform. The young woman who helped type a couple of one's poems, for whom one had written another. The young woman who looked beautiful and sweet in her wedding dress. The young woman who had those three lovely children. The young woman whom one saw a few months before, a picture of health and vitality. How does one wait for the end when one knows she is slipping away, that she is going away soon? How does anyone wait for that to happen? But such is how we are made that so long as one is not removed from the picture, or remove oneself, then wait one must. To say that the wait is painful, excruciating and torturous, is to be terribly banal, bathetic. What one feels during the hiatus is inexpressible, as it should be. Actually it is not something felt, it is beyond affect, void, enveloping deadness. Well, maybe those who can pray will pray at such trying times, but despite the passing fancy that praying may be something considerable in the circumstances, I did not and could not do such a thing during the wait. Oh, I did indeed pray, after a fashion – I hoped, wished, imagined, projected, dreamed, daydreamed, ached, fantasised the possibility of a miraculous cure, of parascientific remission, of hyperphysical rallying, of inexplicable healing. That was all I could do, momentarily, before I was brought to earth again, and then the emotive autopilot had kicked in.

The desire to do a number of things, crucially the will to write, had wilted, the all-but-finished *God Will Not Help Nigeria Until…* remained on ice. I couldn't care less whether God actually decided to help Nigeria, turn the place into the new Promised Land, although I knew deep within me that what I wrote in the article was pretty logical. Once again the reasoning had superimposed itself: if God does not care whether any of his supposed children, even a premoral child like a two-year-old, goes through insufferable pain, why must he care whether or not a country destroys itself? Although I might call myself an agnostic, I tend to remove God from the picture whenever I want to make a clear-headed analysis of anything (which makes me an apatheist, if you please). For instance, how would I begin to infuse God's love and goodness into my ruminations during my sister's illness? Abstracting God often configures my mind, it unclouds my thoughts, it crystallises reality, it allows for better and fairer focussing. While I imagined it would be fine if everyone's prayer suddenly worked and Adejoke miraculously got well, I still allowed myself the space to look at the situation with calm – the likelihood of such prayer having any effect was, in my mind, equal to the odds of God coming round to tell me personally that everything would be fine.

A few months ago I listened to Archbishop of Canterbury, Dr Rowan Williams, holding forth on BBC Radio 4 about how some might turn to or from God in difficult times. Maybe because my decision to question a lot of religious verities was made long ago, I did not find myself musing over this sort of choice when my sister was ill. And while it may be understandable why those who turn away from their belief in God have done so when they are experiencing things that seem to belie God's especial interest in them, I believe one should wait until calmer times to make the decision, not in the heat of the moment, and one might even see, as I did, that God is as irrelevant to one's happiness or bliss as he is in default connected to one's pain or grief. As for those who were not too godly before and have turned to God in hard times, this is also understandable, self-delusory as it might seem to the 'unbeliever' it may be therapeutic. If turning to God could serve as a warm compress for people in various kinds of discomfort, then why not? Although I don't envy those who make that despondent move, I would if I could, and if I knew I would remain abidingly undeceived – or, better, self-deceived. But what I am unyieldingly not-deceived about is that God, if he exists, must be very much inured to appeals and prayers, pretty eccentric and capricious about listening to anything, to anyone.

It was somewhat like the effort I made to distract myself with reading, an effort to ever so slightly block myself from what my sister might be going through. I tried some psycho-philosophical books, especially those written by Jungian scholars. But though they contained helpful insights into what I was experiencing, I couldn't go far with them. I found most prose, however stirring and allusive, heavygoing and discursive. I made an effort to reread a book someone wrote about death but I realised this was a luxury that only someone who is not patently on the home-straight towards a date with death could afford. Although we are all naturally travelling on the crowded featureless road of mortality, it was still debatable whether the bell was at the time loudly tolling for me – it might, doubtless, be pealing and echoing in my direction, but as is sometimes sneakily the case, I could not hear it. In spite of being in this chancy position of aliveness, I could not bring myself to reread the book. Would my sister be able to read even the breezily composed title of the book in the circumstances, a title which ironically trivialises the creepy peremptoriness of death? And what about the author's longish, impersonal, broad-church treatment of the daunting subject, his jaunty almost jocose prose-style? Antic, Attic-witted reflection on the nature of death had no meaning or purpose with the irrepressible realisation that Adejoke might be gone soon, gone away from us, that if by chance I went on to gain longevity, I would never see her again – even if I did outlast by a day, a year, scores of years, I would never see her.

Before she was diagnosed with cancer, when she was still in the throes of what turned out to be 'referred pain' in her leg, my eyes had caught Oliver Sacks' *A Leg to Stand On* on my bookshelf, a book that I bought almost a decade before. When I re-browsed the blurb and saw the book was about how Sacks rallied his way to health after injuring a leg, I got into it, and I was intrigued by the story, the power of the narration, the superb and persuasive teasing-out of the tale, but in places I was almost defeated by Sacks' heavy deployment of gadzookery, so much so that sometimes I forgot I was reading a book written in the final quarter of the 20th century. I don't know what I would have done with the book if I was still reading it when it transpired that what Adejoke had was cancer, that the problem was not in her leg.

At last poetry turned out to be the analgesic. Since I had put aside poem-making as a craft I might yet turn to in salted old age, I had not been reading a lot of poems as I used to do. Poetry's traditional brevity, conciseness and common stylistic valency had gripped me again during the trying period of my sister's illness. Rilke. Yeats. Eliot. Fenton. Yeats, an old favourite, helped more than all. I was able to get into his Collected Works, although not with the exhilarating, fine-spirited elation that I bore around in the days that I first read the Irish sage and mage. Again I wandered into, *'I heard an old religious man but yesternight declare that he had found a text to prove that only God, my dear, could love you for yourself alone and not your yellow hair.'* I was taken by the lines so much that I wished I could find the old man and argue with him that sometimes your loved ones could love you, warts, yellow hair and all, and even if no one would love you in spite of your yellow hair, your dog would, as Schopenhauer found. This was when I realised that I was smouldering, not angry, but peeved, peevish, red-hot embers banked in deep ashes. It was only in such a state that I would dishonour lines by Yeats – I didn't know I would see such a day, not even if he was trying to sell God in a backhanded sort of way.

To a considerable extent, for me art often serves the purpose Arthur Schopenhauer (who lived with his dogs for most of his adult life) says it does serve in relieving the very burden of being an existent, although Schopenhauer's favoured medium, music, did not exactly provide any succour. I had long become a keen listener to baroque/classical music, the sort of music Schopenhauer knew, and I am sure the effect, if I had sought it out to soften the despondency of loss, would be more Spinozist than Schopenhauerian – that is subtly calming, mentally soothing, even metaphysical, it would not have acted as a vehicle for Schopenhauer's will-to-live. Handel's *Hallelujah* chorus, which was lost on me when I was eight or so, had become, more than a dozen years later, one of the most moving pieces of music I ever listened to. *Hallelujah* still tugs at my heartstrings – not the song itself, but the singing, the normally oceanic compass of the delivery, the rapidfire bouncy riffs. But then what would *Hallelujah* avail in my roiled state of mind? (Occasionally I listen to some gospel music, not the American flourish-and-fanfare type, but some of those sung by Nigerians in Yoruba and Igbo. I am still drawn into the easy singalong chirpiness of some of the songs, the percussive traditionalisation of tempo, however the point of listening to them is not pietistic even in the best of times, it is only part of my generic appreciation of music. Again, this sort of music was the last thing I would listen to when I was thinking about my sister.) Peter Gabriel's song about existential entropy, *Downside Up,* came to me a number of times, I even listened to it once or twice on *YouTube*, not with a view to use it as anaesthesia but just to recapture its aphoristic tunefulness.

I do not know and will never know, and will never want to know, what thoughts went through my sister's head in her last days. Resignation and acceptance possibly, but I somehow hoped she had not rejected her God or her Christian religion in the end. I don't know why I feel this way, considering my views about those things; I shouldn't even have cared either way. But this is not about me. Adejoke had spent most of her life believing, and if she began to repine against God in those last hours it would be like a reverse deathbed conversion, which would be pointless. There was so much prayer during Adejoke's illness, a lot of fasting, a lot of beseeching appeals for God's favour, so much God-will-heal-you grace notes, appeals for miracle, for the cauterising power of Paraclete (Holy Spirit or Fire) to intercede, and while I wasn't involved in any of these, I deferred to the sentiments and motives behind them. And there was the small smart voice of Kierkegaard, especially the seductive Christian notionisms of *Sickness unto Death*. Despair is the 'sickness', the necessary malaise of human existence and immanent in despair is God-as-consolation in the same way an oasis, or the shade of the dune, is concomitant with the thirsty aridity and broiling discomfiture of the desert. For those who believe in God, to hang on to him is to subsume their despair within the vast ocean of the will, it signifies floatation, buoyancy, deathlessness. I do understand the gist of Kierkegaard's thesis, I understand it from the angle of someone who thinks that what the Danish philosopher is offering is nothing but a caressing lullaby. But I don't think it mattered to me so long as the physical pain Adejoke went through was mediated by what she believed. Did her faith lessen her pain, would it? Although that would be impossible for both of us to do, if my sister had had the strength, in those last days, to niggle over the finer points Pascal's wager with me, I would gladly have begged her to hedge her bets on the possibility of 'God' being there somewhere, since in Pascal's logic, she would not lose anything, except perhaps a brother whom God might consign to perdition for not believing in him.

I spoke to Adejoke many times during her illness and I always told her, sincerely, that I hoped something would happen to reverse the galloping cancer, because in spite my curiously self-bewildering and vicarious peek into Kierkegaard's transcendent handbag of spiritual therapeutants, I did not really lose my this-worldly footing. I fell back on hope, I hoped against hope, hoped vastly, impossibly, with self-parroting amplitude. The word I used most of the time was Hope. One of the times I spoke to Adejoke, I said to her in a flat fond voice, 'I hope you will pull through this.' Only my sister could wring this kind of hollow self-delusion from me. Because at this point, I didn't need Sartre to tell me that I was hopeless and that I was only 'acting' as if I had any hope. A few days later, for the first time in so many years Adejoke had said to me, now in a heartbreakingly morphine-clouded voice, further strained by telephonic one-dimensionality. 'Pray for me, Ade, don't just hope. Pray for me.' When we disconnected, I slumped on my seat and my eyes smarted, springing tears. To the degree that I had never known before, I knew what Helplessness means, even Hopelessness, and how, even if I believed in any sort of god, it would not have made any blinking difference now.

I remained in this state of maundering mental suspension and emptiness in the days before the life-support machine was finally turned off. The lysis never came – it was controlled crisis all the way. *Adejoke is leaving us*, this was the way I put it to someone who said to me that maybe the power of prayer, the favour-dispensing hand of God, would pull her round. The metastasis was extensive, critical. The pain itself, while dulled with morphine, was agonal. So much so that respite, release, was what I thought I should hope for now, although I could not completely consciously bring myself to do that.

It came to pass anyway, in spite of what I hoped or did not hope for, and there was nothing for it but to accept, to believe that she was gone. In the early days I thought of nothing but my sister – the whole of the 38-odd years had run again and again, circularly, sharply, with one hires sepia picture dissolving into another like in those vintage films. It was all overwhelming, deeply wounding – the sweeping wholesale vista of hindsight was too poignant to plumb, even to glance over. I fought shy of Mnemosyne, the seductress whom Nabokov celebrates and romances in *Speak, Memory*. Speak not, Memory! And the daughters of Mnemosyne, the Muses, were, of course, identically mute, aloof.

Black dwarf: a white dwarf (star) that no longer gives light because all the energy has been used up, having burnt bright for trillions of years. Black dwarf was the phrase which came to my mind a few years before when I heard of the passing of an old friend and classmate, Makinde, who succumbed to a merciless kind of liver dysfunction. When we were in secondary school some 25 years before, Makinde was a repository of energy and vitality, a nonpareil footballer, a peerless sprinter and tireless long-distance runner, an impala-hoofed high-jumper, a self-cannonballing long-jumper, a deft and matchless javelin-thrower, a light-fisted shot-putter, a killer boxer, a past master at karate and an exact kickboxer. Makinde was an all-rounder, he participated in every sport in the school, and any 'house' he belonged in always won all the prizes on school sports day, so most students wished they would find themselves in the same house as Makinde in the yearly lottery shuffling of house-placement. Makinde was the hyper-performing decathlete, the totem of sports glory for both his house and school. He and I were in the same class from year one to five, and we were friends all through the years, but after secondary school I didn't see him for some 15 years until I ran into him in a beer-lounge in the city of Akure a year before I would leave Nigeria. He'd been a civil servant for many years, and had had preferment enough to be able to afford the good life. I remember asking him, teasingly, 'Can you still run as fast?' Of course not. Makinde was now a stoutish man in his early 30s, with a pronounced beer-belly that mocked every suggestion of athleticism. He bought several rounds of beer for me and the friend that I went to the bar with.

As is often the case, Makinde was Akin's friend too, and when my brother told me on the phone that he was dead, what came to my mind was Makinde's restless energy, his electric quickness, his muscly aliveness, all memories of a quarter of a century ago. Even when I saw him in the 'beer parlour', changed and older, just like I would have looked to him too, his bonhomie, his patent enjoyment of the life he was living then, had compensated for what time had done to his adolescent vitality. But then when I heard the news of his death, it was that way in which I knew him long ago that came back, again and again, his livewire incarnation, that whooshing dynamism. And somehow I re-realised how time-consuming and unnecessary it is to dwell on the ephemerality of life, because it is the *thing*. Vita Brevis. In an eyeblink, everything is gone. It is why Adejoke's passing made as much sense as not. Even if all of us seven siblings lived to be hoary centenarians – which would be very much unlikely – I believe in the end I would still have joined Seneca in ruminating on the shortness of life.

I read Fritz Zorn's *Mars* many years ago and it was pretty much inevitable that I would pick out the extraordinary book from my book-shelf again after the death of my sister. The book provided a low-volume, if piquant, incidental music to the grieving *precess*. *Mars* – name of Latin god of war, rage and creativity – survived Zorn's depressive proclivity towards burning his unpublished writings. The book was accepted by a publisher a few days before the young man's death from cancer. And the question may be asked: why pick such a dark book in the circumstances? Far better than rereading something like the 'Book of Job', rereading *Mars*, I daresay, would help (and had helped) me to gain mental ballast in bereavement. As a matter of fact, *Mars* gives me a better 'answer to Job' than Jung's book which purports to do that – in a way, what *Mars* does is tell God, Job and even Jung to fuck off. For some readers, Zorn's self-flagellation and self-hate might grate and the book might become too hard-going, but then one has to look beyond the poor man's melancholy and perverse oversomatisation of cancer, beyond his wistful anger, one must try to get a purchase on the mercurial and subterranean flux of Zorn's emotions as they die away into a trickly ebb.

And there was John Updike's *Endpoint*, a gentler book than *Mars*, released after the great man's death. The poems in the collection, though chiefly about mortality and memory, are as laidback and blithe as only Updike could ever make them. The fascinating thing about *Endpoint* is the acuity of the poet's consciousness of the seepage of time, how he is keenly aware that there is no time to waste, no prosy prolix cruising, no time to spend on intricate weaving and colourful beading of sentences and phrases, how he telescopes all of 76 years into no more than two dozen pages of light psalmic verse, everything shorn of any pompous surreality of religion, in spite of Updike's ever-latent Protestantism.

I may have returned to Updike after my sister's death because of a faint tug of the memory. I have been a loyal reader of Updike for some time and his death was so well-broadcast that it would even be difficult for anyone who had never heard of the man to miss the obituaries. Naturally Updike and *Endpoint* – which I'd bought and had not been able to read – had come back when my sister died. But there was something that rankled too. In 1995 I paid a visit to my sister in Port Harcourt. I stayed a couple of days with her and her family. Before I went to Port Harcourt, I had happened on the last three of James Updike's *Rabbit Quartet* in one of the roadside second-hand booksellers in Lagos (which was where I bought the first Updike book I read many years before). I whiled the journey-time to Port-Harcourt away reading *Rabbit Redux*, and during the time that I stayed in my sister's house I read both *Rabbit is Rich* and *Rabbit at Rest*. I finished the last book in the car as my sister drove me to the bus station on the morning that I would travel back to Lagos. Even now Harry 'Rabbit' Angstrom's death from heart attack remains the most memorable fictional description of an *ending* I have ever read, I surprised myself by being affected by the aging fictional character's death. I was so taken with the final passages of Updike's book that I couldn't follow the chat Adejoke was having with me. Even after I finished it, I was still a bit distracted, automatically rereading the final paragraphs.

'Anything interesting in the book?' it was Adejoke asking, possibly the second time.

'Someone just died, a character—'

I think every writer – or just about anyone – has thought about how whatever mental energy she possesses will cease to function with death, and how people might wonder about books she never got round to writing. And truly there is always a profound sense of vacancy when a writer dies, the feeling that she might have gone on to write millions more words, to achieve great things. When the news of Christopher's Hitchens' cancer broke, I missed it because the transfixing searingness of my own sister's diagnosis took some processing. When I finally heard the sad news it was not so much his books, or whatever books he still had in him, that I imagined I would miss if his cancer was terminal, like Updike's, as his superlative chutzpah as a speaker, his debonair verbal attitude, his ability to clobber and brain his fellow debaters savagely, scalp them and gloatingly hang their hollowed-out skulls on a stick. But even as I write this sentence Hitchens, ill and hairless with chemotherapy, is still hanging anyone who takes on him up dry. Although his books are often engaging, and his presumed swansong, *Hitch 22*, is brilliant and witty, orally Hitchens is doing what Updike did well with the pen – the keyboard, if you like – always allowing for the polar temperaments of both men. It is indeed enjoyable to watch the ailing Hitchens run rings round Tony Blair just as it is uplifting to read Updike at poetic full tilt. In *Endpoint* Updike even dallies with irreligious levity – a final crack at his blanched Lutheranism – declaiming: *All praise be valium in Jesus' name*. But these offerings are a reminder that however long we think we are going to live, however much we think we are immune from death, it dances like a skeleton grinning in the backdrop of our nightly dreams.

Fool that I am I had to bring yet another offspring – third – into this vale of tears, this dale of fears. My wife was months gone when my sister fell ill, and in a curiously self-pillorying case of 'eternal return', as Adejoke trailed away from life, this foetal life in the womb of my wife was bulking, emerging. Of course after I had my first child it was curtains for my fanciful thought of being a practical antinatalist. Naturally a number of things, *reasons*, are to blame for my inability to carry the courage of my conviction: existential reasons, human reasons, animal reasons, even cultural reasons. Like many people who see something in what the great philosopher expounded, my views have been rendered down Schopenhauer-lite. Any kind of hard-headed overrealistic attitudes and perceptions that I had have been mellowed not by any rose-tinted illusions but by a firmer if pliant purchase on the absurdity of the human condition. Sometimes I do ask myself whether I could truly have lived a life like Schopenhauer's even if I tried, I mean the sort of crabbed lifestyle the philosopher lived, now slapped with the 20/21st century patina. Could I have been the secular dog-loving stylite that Schopenhauer was? I guess I could, but then that was never meant to be. However, my fatherhood had not made me lose sight of what the unapologetic antinatalist, David Benatar, calls the 'hurt', the pitfalls, the varying quotients of privative accidents that anyone who brings a child into being also burdens the child with, the physical and moral traps he inadvertently, or carelessly, or even selfishly, ignored as he planned and prepared to bring forth the child – although for many, procreation is an animal thing, merely systemic, something that must be done, planned or unplanned. Even so it makes no difference whether one hopes to spend one's bagfuls of money to sweeten the life of one's offspring or one just cannot give a damn what happens to one's spawn, every child that is born, princess or pauper, will have to live – even if it dies a few moments later, which is possibly good for it, although not so good for its bereaved bringers. And for us who live longer, the problem is not life itself because we all know it is a Janus-faced creature which plays deadpan poker with us with one side of its face and tickles us to death with the other, the Joker side. The problem is living: the repetitive chore of sleep-and-wake, of eat-and-shit, of chase-and-conquest and other fillers and distractions, pleasurable and otherwise.

Between the time of Adejoke's death and my child's arrival I read Benatar's *Better Never to have Been* and I found that it was an incisive exercise in self-echoing 'I told you so'. Although Benatar reckons without God and religion, the argument of the book is as sensible to me as Christopher Hitchens' more polemical and graphic dilations on God – the pointlessness of God. Benatar piles on well-argued truism on truism (and so many uneasy truths), *pure* commonsense on commonsense, so much so that by the time I finished the book all I could do was put it aside and try to forget antinatalism for some time while I waited for the birth of my child, a boy. *I have to put my mind in antenatal mode now*, I said to myself. After all, as Benatar points out, the unborn child knew absolutely nothing about why he had to be born, so I would not deprive him the attention he needed. And why not simply face up to the thoughtless earthbound ego-trip which informed the act of procreating and the lack of commitment to allowing my views on antinatalism to flower and bear the fruits of childlessness?

I sat beside the anaesthetist and watched the 'happy event' in the birth chamber. There was a CD player in the theatre and before the section commenced, the anaesthetist had asked my wife and I whether we would like some music as an accompaniment to the arrival of the baby. My noncommittal shrug was nullified by my wife's gentle affirmation. I noticed that we were not asked the kind of music we would like to listen to and in the seconds before the anaesthetist/deejay turned on the CD, I thought it was going to be a late aubade provided by Vivaldi or Schubert or Mozart – wasn't there the *in utero* spinoff of the 'Mozart effect?' For some time the idea has been sold that foetuses listen to music in the womb and usually what compilers think these unborn babies would find listenable was a miscellany of instrumental music, anything from Beethoven's *Bagatelle* in A to just about anything by the incredible John Williams, but it is often the older vintage that makes the collection. Besides the new-ageish belief that the music would make the baby to be restful and well-adapted to its oceanic surrounding, some mothers had infused the idea of playing music for their foetuses with a kind of tantric sense of the child really enjoying the music, understanding it, plumbing the complex depths of it. The very fact of listening to the music had conferred on it genius-level intelligence, and even if the listening stopped immediately after birth – as it often does – it would not matter. (What would music by the likes of Beyonce and Rihanna do to the baby, if it were a boy, say?) But what came on was Rod Stewart's version of *Father and Son* – which I suspected was not a coincidence. It wasn't clear that my wife, who agreed to an accompaniment of music, could actually listen to it, cumulatively wearied with the unwieldy burden of pregnancy and distracted with anticipation, she only nodded slightly when I asked whether she liked the song. I couldn't have been attentive to the music for more than half a minute before it fizzled into a Muzak baffle. The Muzak effect.

I was hoping it would all go well, that both mother and baby would be all right. Since it was a scalpelled delivery, I could sense the slicing and snipping going on, the stemming and stanching, the cleaning, the cutting. There was the machine, ticking and tocking: one ignores the machine and its ominous screen, the marginal porpoising, the little trickly lifts and rhythms of lines on the screen. But then I could whisper to the wife in her state of birthing stupor – although clearly dazed, she knew what was going on. The first time around, eight years before, I had seen far more gore and Caesarean shambles. By the time the third came, the observing partner had been carefully and thoroughly screened off, possibly because some fathers-to-be were said to have swooned while sitting in on the operation. Besides being left to comfort one's partner in chromosomal splicing, one also saw the surgeons and midwives at work. And one could see the baby when it was brought out, skimmed with vernix, trailing umbilical cord. And the wah-wahing. It was the cries of the baby boy which brought it to me that the music had long stopped playing, the only track that I could recall playing was the first one, *Father and Son*.

There was, again, the ritual of christening. My first child, my only daughter, has all of eight names, of which I didn't give her any. In a chivalrous kind of way, I had deferred to my mother: the name she sent from Nigeria is my daughter's first name. During conception, when we discovered that she was a girl, I had hoped to call her Mojisola, my late big sister's name. But ultimately one of the two names Mother sent, Omotola, which meant pretty much the same thing as Mojisola, stuck. And the other names? My mother-in-law sent three names. My wife gave her three. Seeing all this, it is clear there is no bucking tradition and kin consensus when a child is born, and London is as close to 'home' as can be. This is why I was also relaxed about having a pastor coming round to conduct the naming ceremony. Even if his benedictions and prayers meant nothing to me, it meant a lot to most of those who came for the ceremony. Plus if I can listen to gospel music and enjoy the strains of its musicality and brio, or nod and hum to the more memorable hymns, if I can marvel at the beauty and magnificence and the masonic as well as artistic genius that went into the creation of cathedrals, why not let a pastor make solemn declamations of wishful thinking on the day my child was given a name?

Months after my daughter was born, she took her first step and this had called forth the Muse of Poetry, a presence who now rarely visited. I wrote the first poem in two years. Here is *On My Daughter's First Step*:

With novel deliberation and a lack of poetry
she lifts a leg, the right one. Now
this is it, she has taken the first step, and like Yeats
I offered up a prayer to my daughter...
May your walk grow steady and sturdy, in time.
May you be guided by the strength of your own will.
Do not burden yourself with more than your feet
can carry. Stride if you can – stroll, swagger, shimmy.
Remember that a foothold is better than a toehold.
There was this drunken prayer from the old campus
Cult of Bacchus: 'Walk and Never Stumble' – but
if you stumble, stub your toe right, the sinister side,
for Mother Luck.
Allow for legroom, your legs' room,
vote wisely with one foot and veto sensibly
with the other. Be sure-footed even while wearing
high heels (because I'd truly be sad to see
you keel over while voguing through the catwalk).
Do not follow in the footsteps of the ancient
eastern women who bound
and minified their feet to please their lords,
I tell you even if they grow to be size ten,
modern lords, tycoons, dukes and dudes would
build a shrine around them.
Crevices of cold kibes and excrescences
of corn? Well, guide against them.
And please always
remember the cliché of the heel of Achilles

and gods who possess feet of clay.
Oh, now she totters, no, she toddles...she dodders
Like an old woman cramped with age,
On her last legs.

My second child, a boy, is called Adebayo. When I told a neighbour my son's name, the gentleman asked whether I named him after the Togolese international, Emmanuel Adebayor. Well, nothing can be farther from the truth. I do not watch a lot of league football, or shall we say, club-based football, I only watch, if I can, tournaments like Africa's Cup, European Cup or the World Cup. Although, curiously, a Nigerian acquaintance named his son after Beckham's son, Brooklyn, I do not like football well enough to honour my child with the name of any of its players, not even if he belonged to a team that brought the World Cup to England – or Nigeria. For one thing, my son's name does not have the consonant 'r' at the end – a needless Gallicism. The boy was named after my late father. The backstory to the decision to call my son my dad's name is a sentimental one, it is also a function of a lingering cosiness with depth psychology, a figurative compounding of the names of Freud and Jung, accented with a shuffle of their ideas on dreams. Because in a dream I saw my late father lying with upturned face on a kind of rug in an empty room, and suddenly a baby appeared at the side of his grizzled head, tousling the hair with its tiny hand. As I watched, the old man signed to me to take the child. I leaned over to pick up the tot, then I woke up. A few weeks later it transpired that my wife who had not been able conceive – to my undisguised relief – for almost seven years discovered that another life was growing in her. A not unwelcome piece of news if you ask me, and in spite of myself I could not disconnect the dream from what came after it. All right, this is stretching causality a bit, but when I told my mother about this rather translucent dream she made the connection fast and suggested something to the effect that if the child, still an embryonic speck, turned out to be a boy, we might as well call him any of the late old man's names. Hence, Adebayo. But as if the Fates were bent on ridiculing my smouldering, now well-and-truly defunct, pretensions to being an antinatalist, a few months after the arrival of Adebayo, another little seed implanted itself in what it saw as its natural habitat.

A week after the newborn boy came – months after the passing of Adejoke – the naming ritual was repeated. A lot of people were snowed in that early December morning and only core family members and the inevitable pastor turned up. My Yoruba ancestors might include, *He who comes with snow*, or maybe, simply 'Snow' amongst the names of the baby. Besides the fact that my ancestors might not care so much about snow, calling someone a name that recalls or commemorates an event or a day is still common in Yorubaland. Now no one gave Akin, my brother, the name 'Sunday' when he was born, but since he was born on the day some people started to call him that and it caught on so much that for almost a quarter of a century he answered to Sunday. As it happens, someone jestingly suggested 'Snow' as one of the many ancillary names the newborn should be given. But I was only interested in giving him no more than one name and it was not Snow. I left the invention of the remaining eight or so to his mother and others.

Days earlier, when my wife was compiling the names for the tot, she had written 'Adejoke' among the lot. This is essentially, and even strictly, a girl's name, it is like giving a boy the name Rebecca or Sarah (not an impossibility, I used to think Evelyn could only be a girl's name until I knew Evelyn Waugh) I would have wondered why my wife went so far off the tangent if I didn't know her motive. If I would not call my daughter Ruth or Rebecca, for instance, there was no reason I would call her Princess Tiara, Harper Nine, Malusha or Laneesha. Or call my male child Prince Diadem. Simple straightforward names which made no grand claims were just fine. In spite of the genderfuck inherent in giving my son Adejoke, it is a simple and straightforward name – even more so. My son came five months after the death of my sister and what preoccupied me during the time of his conception was the illness and death of my sister. So if the boy should be called anything in a complementary and commemorative way, it should be Adejoke. If we had had a girl, the likelihood was that she would be called my late sister's name and beyond mere name-giving she might be seen, not least by Mother, if not exactly as Adejoke reincarnate, then as the fruit of the spiritual bond between Adejoke and her brothers and sisters. Possibly, this might have inspired an essay (maybe a poem now, the Muse might be back) that would explore rebirth and reincarnation and how this would only be tiny comfort, even if such things were possible. Having a child and losing a sister one has known for all of 38 years are two different, separate, not to say disparate, things, and it is better not to compare – or contrast – the elemental feelings and emotions which almost entirely rend the two events apart. Here is the truth: there is no replacing my sister, not even with a baby boy whose future is as obscure and unknowable as that of the beautiful baby girl I saw in the cradle when Adejoke was born. Although he is going to live his own life, dream his own dreams, experience his own joys and pains, I could not find any reason why the newborn boy should not be called Adejoke.

Perhaps it would work better if malaria was damned and spat upon, although just as in the case of Death and Comet, if it served any purpose at all it would be that of poetry, of art. Malaria as art? Well, I dealt with malaria in a mildly sinister children's story I wrote in which a mosquito cajoles a young girl to lift the net that protects her against it. The tiny creature begs the girl, sings for her, dances for her, takes the shape of a fairy. So much so that the little girl of seven finally lifts the net and allows the mosquito and its hidden friends in. They attack her, pinprick her with their proboscides, suck her blood, she falls sick but gets well after a few days of treatment and rest. The story ends with another mosquito arriving at the net over the bed of the little girl, buzzing, directly metamorphosing into a fairy. Ultimately, in the sketch, mosquito was more in evidence than malaria – or are they one and the same thing, should the anopheles be defined solely in the guise of malaria? What use is that morbific flying insect?

Possibly the story was another way of dealing with my sister's death. Although these spectral vectors of death were almost everywhere in the night air I grew to dread and fear even a single mosquito bite, far more than the resulting malaria. I had had my fair share of the awful disease. My first and only experience of journeying into a trancelike state was when I was about five and I had malaria, the fever got so high and convulsive that I still vaguely remember how I glimpsed figures ranging from huge winged angels, through monstrous masqueraders, to a million twinkling cat's eyes. I spent a couple of days in the private clinic of Father's doctor friend where I rallied fast. And there was another memorable experience I had of being sick with malaria. I was about 13. At its onset I took the first four dose of chloroquine and a couple of febrifugal pills, I then lay down on my bed, hot and slightly discomfited, there was an undercurrent of chills and a soft tremor. The medicine I took possibly had some effect after a while, my temperature levelled from broiling hot to simmering hot, the chills and tremor seemed to have abated, but I knew well enough that this was only the start of malaria, it was yet to peak, it might take some four days or more for the medicines to restore me to health. To pluck myself out of the abyssal spaciness that malaria seems to bring on, I struggled up, picked a copy of Hemingway's *Old Man and the Sea* that I had been held back from reading by a glut of fast-paced crime fiction I had buried myself in since I discovered the genre a couple of years before. *Old Man* was the first book by Hemingway that I read and the first 'serious' or literary novel. Months before, I had hesitantly taken Rex Warner's *The Aerodrome* from my father's pared-down bookcase and had found it surprisingly engaging.

Reading *Old Man and the Sea* was a different matter, it smacked almost of a spiritual experience. In spite of the feverishness, the minor astigmia induced by the fever and a gentle achy throbbing in the temple of my head, I finished the book in just an hour and a half, taking in both the story and its meaning with singular clearsightedness, and as I read it seemed as if I was with the old man in his fishing boat, at sea, adrift, buffeted, jaded. I fell asleep after reading the book just as the old man at the end of the story. I dreamt too, not of a lion on an African seaside but of being washed up on a cool, palmy shore. I woke a couple of hours after sinking into malarial slumber, the bed sheet sodden with sweat. I was sweating out the fever, Father would say. I indeed felt better, temperature down, pulsating headache gone, the bitter/metallic taste in the mouth that comes with ague almost normalised, my head the clearest it had been for years. It was as if a patron saint, an angel of health and healing, had arrived while I slept and had censed the